An "A" Effort

Matthew Tyler Giobbi, Ph.D.

D1495269

DEDICATION

This book is dedicated to my students
—*past, present, and future.*

CONTENTS

ACKNOWLEDGMENTS

I have learned much from the nearly 5,000 students whom I have taught over the past 10 years, and I wish that I could acknowledge every one of them by name. Of those former students, the following have thoughtfully contributed ideas directly to this book:

Shawn Scott, Pam Prather, Jane Kohn, Guadalupe Mercado, Stephanie Macias, Tennille Smith, Makeda Alexander, Rena Lunzer, Gina Trapano, Latonda Hinton, Jennifer Irving, Fanta Keita, Travis Logan, Samir Khawaja, Sali Ali, Guadalupe Merino, Jessica Melendez, Legouaze James Joseph, Kristina De Pinto, Mikhail Job, Christopher Fuentes, and Gerri Benjamin, Shelley Robinson, Ronald Kulwatdanaporn, Robert Snyder, Linda Barlow, Tiffany Esparra, Erykah Jones, Jacqueline Ford, and Gregory "G.P." Parker.

I would also like to thank Dori Seider, Henry MacAdam, Christopher Minnich, Eric Doney, Jim Gloria, Alvyn Haywood, Andrew Conrad, Susan Zambrio, Vincenzo Di Nicola, Gregory Bray, Robert Craig Baum, Gerard La Morte III, and Conchur De Barra for their tireless support, professional guidance, and encouragement.

To my parents, Robert and Charlotte, who have always encouraged me to follow my heart, even in the most fantastic endeavors.

INTRODUCTION

"A man is relieved and gay when he has put his heart into his work and done his best; but what he has said or done otherwise shall give him no peace."

-Ralph Waldo Emerson

By my senior year of college, I had managed to support myself by teaching. Although I had not yet received my graduate degree, or my first college teaching position, I was earning enough money to live by giving private music lessons and tutoring first year students at the university's learning center. During that year, before going off to graduate school, I got my first glimpse into how both *successful* and *unsuccessful* college students approach their work and study, how they take exams, and how they manage their academic obligations.

Sitting down, one-on-one, with undergraduates (sometimes for ten hours per day), I gained insight and experience into where students go right—and where they can go wrong—in university studies. If you are an undergraduate senior who intends to become a college professor or teacher, I recommend that you take a job at your university's tutoring center. The lessons you learn will be invaluable.

During those long days of tutoring, I found that students who were struggling in school were typically making a handful of very similar mistakes. Most of the students were unprepared for the challenges and demands of college academics. In many cases it was a simple matter of introducing the student to reading comprehension, listening, note taking, test taking, and paper writing techniques. Within a few weeks I watched most of my students' grades go from below average and average, to above average. The scenario became so familiar to me that I could offer just a few, prescribed ideas to students and their performance would increase by an entire letter grade within one test period.

It wasn't long before word got around that I had a powerful technique for struggling psychology students. That reputation followed me, when, two years later, after earning my master's degree, the very same university offered me my first teaching position.

I have an intuitive sense of how to explain complicated ideas in understandable ways. I was aware of being able to do this since childhood, when I would pretend to teach imaginary classes how to do everything from drawing comics to playing the drums.

It has been ten years since I taught my first college course and longer than that since I was a tutor at the college learning center. In that time I have encountered thousands of students, of all ability, interest, enthusiasm, and skill levels. I have learned so much *from* my students, more than I ever could have learned *as* a student. I attempt in every class that I teach to pass on ideas, attitudes, and techniques that students can use in any course. I have always been more interested in helping others to fulfill their dreams and potential than whatever it was that I was teaching.

I have learned that it all boils down to this: if you want to become an "A" student, to see your name listed with academic honors, and if you want to know that you have done your absolute best in any course, you need to make school your number-one priority. I mean this. Regardless of whatever your responsibilities are outside of school, regardless of what you love to do for fun, you must rein it in, set boundaries with it (and others), and make it clear that the decision to go to college means that, at least for the next four-years, college is *the* priority.

If you are not willing to make that statement, or if you truly are unable to, you need to examine if this is a good time to attend college. If you are a non-traditional student with family demands, is now the time to go to college full-time, or is it better to take one course per semester? If you are a traditional student who has just graduated from high school, and will be living on your own for the first time, is your priority set on social or academic life? If you are one of those who are able to balance social and academic priorities successfully, then put down this book, you do not need it. But if you are not getting the kind of grades that you would like to get, or if you want to make sure that your transition into college academics is as smooth as possible, then keep reading—this book is for you!

Some students are great in class discussions, writing papers, and then earn below-average scores on their exams. If this describes you, skip directly to the chapters on studying (Chapter 3) and test taking (Chapter 4). If you feel like you are walking around in a dark room when it comes to writing a paper, you need to go directly to Chapter 5 and get help fast! Of course, return to the beginning of the book and read the rest of it. Most of the information generalizes well to any skill that you want to improve.

The book not only presents my ideas about learning, test taking, paper writing, and memorization, but also presents words of wisdom from my former students. I asked them, "What are the three things that you learned, the hard way, that every college freshman should know?" Can you guess the top three suggestions that over 1,000 of my former students made? I'll build up to number one: 3. Go to class, 2. Read the book, and 1. the number one piece of advice from my former students to freshmen: "Don't party."

This isn't going to be a book about the vices of drugs, alcohol, sex, and college party life. In fact, if the "successful life" is what you are after (jet-setting on the Riviera, living the celebrity-life kind of stuff) then partying might be just what you should be doing. Some research shows that many highly successful and highly powerful professionals were heavy partiers and socialites in college. But I am not so convinced that that tells the whole story. And for most of us, this approach is just not an option.

No, this book is not about telling you not to have fun for four years. This is a book that will give you insight into how to study, read, write, and work more effectively and more efficiently in college. It will give you the insider's edge on how to get the grades that you want, and how to enjoy the process of getting them. Far from a book of "don'ts" this is a book of "dos." This is a collection of ideas that, if used, will give you results by your next exam. But let me stop before I become like a commercial.

I hope that the lessons in this book work as well for you as they have for the students whom I have tutored, taught, and counseled over the past ten years. Good luck and do your best!

Matthew Tyler Giobbi
New York City
March 2012

1 IN THE CLASSROOM

"We aim above the mark to hit the mark."
-Ralph Waldo Emerson

Change your seat & change your self

If there is one thing that I have noticed over the past ten years of college teaching, it is that students who sit in the front row tend to do better on papers, exams, and presentations than those who sit in the back or off to one of the sides of the classroom. Now, I am not saying that sitting in the front row will *make* your grades improve, but I am saying that there is something about an "A" student that makes them *want* to sit in the front row.

From the professor's point of view, the front row students get the most attention. You are only feet away from us, and often our eyes are looking directly to you as we speak. It is not unusual for me to quickly learn the names of the students who sit closest to the front. This, I believe, is because they are the most likely to participate in class, thus making themselves more memorable.

Front row students are typically more engaged with the lecturer and seem to be better note takers too. It is not uncommon to see fewer students taking notes the farther back the aisle one goes. This being said, I should point-out that I was never a first row student. Although my grades were outstanding throughout undergraduate and graduate school, I always preferred to be in the back, or middle, of a classroom. Each of one of us is different, sometimes anxiety and nervousness makes the back row more bearable. However, if you have never tried the front row, give it a go! Even if for just one lecture, try out the point of view from the front, you might discover something wonderful.

Gina, a behavioral science major at Mercy College, described the day she became a "front-row" student:

> "I had never sat in the front row before; I usually liked to stay in the back of the class where no one could see me. Then I went to a 'college success' talk where the speaker told us to sit in the front row. Since my grades weren't so hot, I decided to try it. It was AMAZING! Not only did my grades increase, but, I felt different in the front of the class. I actually started to *feel* like an 'A student'–before I even got the 'A' on my exam!"

Gina is describing something that psychologists have talked about for years. It is called *self-verification theory*, and it goes like this: we often view ourselves in the reflection of others. When people look at us in a positive, praise-worthy way, we often feel good about ourselves and live up to that image. The opposite is also true. When we are looked down upon, or treated poorly, we react with negative feelings like anger, resentment, and self-doubt. When Gina decided to sit in the front row she defined herself to the professor and to her classmates, as a "front-row" student. Her classmates and professors began acting differently towards her, and it wasn't long before she started acting (and feeling) differently about herself. She became a product of her environment, an environment that she shaped for herself.

The power of a smile

Speaking of being nervous, have you ever considered that your professors are often nervous too? Yes, we sometimes are, especially on the first class meeting. Seeing a new student offer a smile helps my nerves to calm on that first day. It is like the student is telling me that they are happy to be meeting me. The one thing that you can always do to make sure that you are remembered and noticed in class is to smile! That's it—just smile at your professor. When you smile, it tells us the same thing that our smile tells you: I am interested in what you are saying, and I am happy to be here. Sometimes when we are concentrating or thinking about difficult material we forget to smile. That's okay! However, being aware of how much a smile can do for you, and your professor, is worth its weight in gold. Research consistently shows that people who smile not only increase their chances of getting what they want out of life, but also tend to have fewer obstacles. Developing a sincere and healthy smile is one of the best things you ever do for yourself, and it's contagious–just try it!

Let me tell you about a former student named Megan. Megan was a first-year student at a community college in Pennsylvania. Although Megan was very bright and friendly, she had few friends and found herself in frequent confrontation with others. The thing that Megan was completely unaware of was her body language and facial expressions. I was initially stupefied when Megan would grimace in disgust, shooting looks of contempt towards me when certain ideas were talked about in class. It was in that introduction to psychology class that Megan realized something that changed her life.

One afternoon we were learning about the basic counseling techniques of nonverbal communication. We explored the importance of becoming aware of our facial expressions when listening to a patient, so that we encourage an open and safe atmosphere for the individual to explore their emotions and relationships. If you have ever watched therapists in action, you will notice that they are careful to maintain an approving and kind demeanor, so that the patients feel safe to say whatever is on their mind.

As students offered interpretations of photographed facial expressions, I noticed a look of awe on Megan's face. She had realized something about herself, and that class was the last time Megan twisted her face in disgust when she didn't agree with or understand something. It wasn't long before a big, natural smile began to appear on Megan's face.

Taking Notes

I encourage my students *not* to take notes. Yes, that is right; my students are greeted on the first day of class with an invitation to put down their pens and pencils and *get into* the conversation. I also encourage them to draw pictures of what we are discussing.

You see, research has shown that for many students note taking actually *interferes* with class participation and comprehension. That's right, taking notes might actually be doing you harm! When we take notes we are engaging the left side of the brain, which is the hemisphere that is also attempting to make sense of the professor's lecture. There is only so much the brain can do at once (multitasking) and *interference* is inevitable. When we stop taking notes and start listening we become engaged in the discussion and are less likely to miss important thoughts.

Drawing is another way of engaging the entire brain. *Visual note taking* is what I call it. We draw and process nonlinearly on the right side of the brain. Allowing the left side to remain in the conversation, while the right side engages with the information, is called *fully engaged* thinking. The key here is to focus all learning styles together: *auditory, verbal, visual,* and *tactile,* through listening, participating, and drawing schematics.

While in college I never took notes in class. I did, though, record each lecture, and then take notes from the recording, after the class. For me, class time was an occasion of engagement with the professor. Give this technique a try—record the lecture, remain engrossed in the classroom discussion, and take notes from the recorded lecture at home. Just make sure that you ask your professors' permission before recording them; we do have the right to say no. Most professors, you will find, will be happy to accommodate your request.

Timing is everything

The best time to make your notes from the lecture recording, and to organize these notes with your reading notes, is within a few hours after the class. In the first few hours after the lecture, the information is still fresh in your mind and the brain continues processing information at an unconscious level.

I recommend typing out handwritten notes onto the computer and saving the document by chapter or topic. You can then integrate your reading notes and website links into the word document. Some students use software that allows them to record the lecture through the text document. This allows you to align text with audio.

I sometimes make hyperlinked study guides for my students as well as embedding videos at critical points in the text. Students report that this enhances their studying effectiveness and it also allows me to make connections with media outside of the textbook.

The most important thing to remember is that the few hours just after your class is the critical period for making your notes.

Asking Questions

It has often been said that there are no stupid questions. I agree with this statement and have found that most questions are of interest to the entire classroom of students, many of who are relieved that *someone* asked!

College is difficult and many of the concepts are new and abstract. Asking questions will help you to process and to *wrap your mind around a topic*. It is important to remember that timing is everything. Make sure that your question is relevant to what is being discussed, and that it is not interrupting the professor's *flow of thought*. In other words, wait for your professor's thought to conclude before raising your hand.

As a student I found it helpful to write my questions down and ask them when the professor paused for questions. Getting into the habit of jotting down your questions will not only benefit your learning, it will also make your classmates and professors grateful to you for not interrupting the lecture.

Smaller colleges have twenty to thirty students in one class. At larger universities you might be one of several hundred students in an auditorium. Asking your professor a question is the perfect opportunity to become an individual, rather than just another face in the crowd. Students who do the best are often the students who go out of their way to engage their professors. However, make sure that you are asking sincere and substantive questions. You don't want to be *that* student, you know, the one who asks questions that are of no use to anyone but him or herself. Make sure that the questions you ask in lecture are questions pertaining to the subject of discussion. Questions regarding *your* absence or *your* exam score are best asked during office hours or in an E-mail.

Those who are in their second, third, or fourth year of college can become easily agitated by some of the first-year students' questions. Sometimes college freshmen have not learned a very important lesson regarding *what* to ask the professor, and unless they have read this book, they will have to learn it the hard way–through a professor's irritation. The lesson is this: there is a time-honored protocol when it comes to asking the professor a question.

What is this protocol? I would say that eight out of ten of the questions asked by students could have easily been answered by looking at the syllabus. If you are repeatedly told, "check the syllabus" when asking your professors a question, it is time to reconsider your questions! Exam dates, reading assignments, grading, and guidelines are all clearly provided for you on the class syllabus. If you cannot find the information you are looking for on the syllabus, then it is best to ask your classmates first. Sometimes there will be a graduate assistant to ask questions on course mechanics. Only after you have exhausted these steps should you ask the professor. Keep your questions for the professor to the course content, not the course mechanics. It is only a matter of consideration and self-sufficiency.

If you decide to E-mail a question to your professor give him or her a few days to respond. Typically a professor is teaching well over one hundred students per semester, in three or more different courses. Always sign your E-mails with your first and last name, as well as the specific class that you are in. It is always a good idea to address your professor as "Dr." or "Professor." Remember that your professor might be teaching more than one section of a class, so include your class meeting time.

It is often best to save more detailed questions for the professor's office hours. Asking before or after the class is typically too rushed and too hectic for a thorough answer. It is best to avoid the mad rush to the desk that often occurs when the professor arrives for the lecture or when the professor is leaving for next lecture.

Take it from Makeda, a senior in New York City, who said, "Never be afraid to ask a question, or to tell the professor when you don't understand –*that's what they are paid for!*" It's true; we are paid to answer your questions.

Reading before the lecture

Without hesitation I offer you this solid piece of advice: do the assigned readings *before* the lecture. Professors are overjoyed when a student asks a question or makes a comment based on the assigned reading. Not only are you going into the lecture with insight into the topic, you are showing your professor that you care about the class.

Reading before the lecture allows you to more easily comprehend the professor's discussion and to think about the lecture in a more penetrating way. Often the professor assumes that you did the assigned readings and conducts the lecture at a more substantive level than a mere introduction to the material. Watch the expression on your professor's face when your question includes a reference to the reading. Try it once and you will be hooked!

Know where your professor left off

"Where did we leave off?" Here are words that every college student will become *very* familiar with. Most students (and professors) have only a vague idea of where in the lecture the last class ended. This is partly because professors are often giving the same lecture two, possibly three, times per week, and typically forget to jot down exactly where they stopped in a particular class. For most students, the days that have passed since the previous lecture were filled with so many tasks, that they are usually at a loss to recall anything about the last lecture. It sometimes feels like every class is the first day of class.

But there is always that one student who saves the day by telling the professor exactly where the class stopped in the previous lecture. Frequently he or she will quote verbatim "you said that today we were going to finish _____ and start _____." How do they do it? Is their memory *that* good? Typically their memory is no better than yours or mine, but their *conscientiousness* is.

Have you ever applied for a job using an online application form? If you have you will recall answering seemingly endless questions about your preferences, likes, dislikes, and attitudes. Human Resource professionals rely on personality tests to determine which applicants will be best for the company and the job. One of those traits that the hiring professionals are looking for is *conscientiousness*.

Defined by psychologists as representing the qualities of efficiency, organization, achievement, and duty, applicants who score high on this trait are typically the best employees. Above all other qualities, the hardware or office supply chain is looking for applicants who are going to show-up for work on time, do an accurate and thorough job, and take pride in their performance. Considered in this way, being a college student is really training you to be a successful job applicant.

The student who is able to tell the professor exactly where he or she left off *conscientiously* jotted down the professor's concluding remarks is anticipating that the professor will be asking for the information at the start of the next class. These students don't possess a special memory gift; they are simply reading it off of their notes—and making a positive impression that the professor will remember them by. The special gift they hold is one they fostered for themselves —*conscientiousness*.

Making Friends in Class

One final thought about the classroom: make a good friend. Fanta, a psychology major from New Jersey, told me, "Try to make friends in your class so that you have someone to study with and to help you keep on track with assignments." Having a study companion and ally in the classroom is invaluable. When you have difficulty understanding a concept, forget when the assignment is due, or need a copy of the notes from a class that you missed, a classroom friend will prove to be a great asset. A word of warning from one former student, Guadalupe, "Choose your friends wisely: look for a partnership of mutual benefit–not one of personal agenda!" Well said.

Shawna, a senior in her final semester, put it succinctly:

"The best lesson I learned in college was studying with other students. I didn't know that there was more than one way to study. I used to waste time trying to learn things the hard way, and then I studied with a group. I figured out from others the best way for me to study."

Shawna has it right. Studying with others not only makes studying more enjoyable; it also helps you to stick to a study schedule. Whether you have a "study buddy" or are part of a larger study group, meeting with others at a regular time to study keeps you on track and will expose you to different study methods. It is also a great way to make friends.

Group Projects

Sometime in your first year of college you are going to be required to participate in a group project. Most of the students that I have spoken with loathe group projects.

Why? Ask "A" students and they will tell you that group projects drag down the quality of their work and require that one or two members of the group compensate for the sub-par work of other group members. The two best students of the group do most of the work in group projects.

There is no way of getting out of group projects, but there are some ways to make sure that your experience is a good one. Here are a few tips on how to make your group experience the best it can be.

In every group there are a few archetypes. There are the two who love to use project time for idle chatter about parties and television. There is the quiet kid who seems to be hanging on for dear life. Finally there is one or two excellent, well-organized, "A" students, one of which is a non-traditional student. Okay, it isn't always like this, but you get the picture I am drawing.

The goal is to be one of the excellent, well-organized students, and not one of the others. Whether you are leading the group or taking a supporting role, you want to pay attention, stay focused, do the best work you can do, and submit it to the group on time.

Nothing is worse than having a student in a group who forces the others to do all of the work. Make sure that you always contribute your share, and don't freeload!

The first question that will be asked is, "Who is the leader of this group?" It might not be overtly discussed or voted on, but within the first few minutes of the group's initial meeting, an organizer will emerge. It happens every time.

Sometimes more than one person will vie for the leadership position. If this happens, hope that the two competitors will make room for co-leadership and not bring the group down with ego trips.

Once a leader emerges it will be necessary to plan the project. If no one seems to be rising to the leadership role, then it's your time to take the rudder. Here are some ideas to help you to be a great project leader.

Make sure that you have a notepad and pen, and assign someone to take notes. Do not take notes yourself; that will give the impression that you are going to do all of the work. This first act of appointing a note-taker is essential as it sets the tone that you are willing to lead the group, but not willing to do the work for the group.

It is best to ask someone if he or she would please take notes, rather than ordering to do so. The student will usually say yes when asked, so there is really no need to make a demand.

The first thing that you should do as the group's leader is ask the members to introduce themselves. Ask them to each tell their name and a little bit about themselves. This will give you a chance to evaluate what and whom you are dealing with. Be aware during this activity; you are gathering vital information on how to go about leading this group. As individuals introduce themselves, have the note-taker record their full name and contact information. You will need to know whom they are and how to reach them if you want to lead a successful group.

Next, you want to clearly state the objective of the group. Have the note-taker write it down on the pad. "The goal of this group is to _____" makes a good starting point. Next, you want to describe some initial positions that need to be decided upon. Depending on the nature of the project, you will have to arrive at a group position on the project's topic. This means that group members will have to voice their opinion.

A word of warning: avoid the clichéd technique called *brainstorming*. This technique is not only irritating to all involved, it is a waste of time. *Brainstorming* is a word that kills intuitive thought. This is not simply my opinion; researchers have clearly shown that the best ideas come from *individuals* and *not groups*. Instead of harassing the group members with an enforced *brainstorming* session, ask them to go home and think about the question at hand. Have them commit to present their thoughts at the next group session. And make sure it is written down by the note-taker.

Having each member think on his or her own eliminates the two biggest pitfalls of group work: *social loafing* and *groupthink*. Social loafing refers to the members who let the others answer all of the questions, come up with all of the ideas, and do all of the work. Don't give group members the opportunity to become social loafers.

Groupthink is the phenomenon that occurs while *brainstorming* together. When people think as a group, their ideas become homogenized and the likelihood for original thought diminishes. By asking members to think at home, on their own, and then report their ideas to the group, you will increase the number of quality and original ideas. This is much more effective than *brainstorming*.

That should take up the first group session. Before leaving, tell each member to check his or her E-mail for the notes from the session, which you will send to them within the day. It is important that you maintain this contact and establish an individual rapport with each group member.

At the beginning of the next group, ask the members to report their ideas. It is important to begin with a group member who you know will set the bar for this. If you begin with a group member who didn't do the work, it will create a negative tone for the group. Look around, who has notes ready to discuss? That's the person to begin with!

The remainder of the group leadership duties will be to assign tasks and deadlines. Always make sure that each member has a definite task and a definite deadline. Be certain that the note taker records each member's task and deadline, and that the assignments are included in the notes that will be E-mailed to all members. In other words, make sure that each member's assigned task is publicly visible to all group members. This simple act will increase the likelihood that they will complete the task.

By the way, it is a good idea to rotate the role of note taker. Make sure that each group member takes a turn at this duty. It will set the precedent of the democratic dynamic.

With a little practice, experience, and advice, you will be able to run a well-functioning group, which will avoid frustration and the chances of *you* doing all of the work for the group.

2 OUTSIDE THE CLASSROOM

"We gain the strength of the temptation we resist."
-Ralph Waldo Emerson

The average college student spends fifteen hours-per-week in lecture, seminar, or lab. This means that nearly seventy-percent of a college student's time is spent outside of the classroom. Today it is a rare luxury for a student to divide that time between social and academic pursuits.

According to the American Council of Education, eighty-percent of college students work at least twenty hours per week. This means that for the majority of college students, more time is spent in the workplace than in the lecture hall. The increasingly monumental financial demands of obtaining a college degree, from board and books to tuition, are leaving today's college student with an immense amount debt and, sadly, little time to make the most out of their years of college. Despite these circumstances, some students are able to not only work full-time jobs, but also raise a family and still maintain excellent grades. Their secret?

They sacrifice a small pay-off today for a bigger pay-off tomorrow.

Holding off for the bigger pay-out

In 1972, Stanford University professor Walter Mischel conducted one of the most famous psychology studies of the Twentieth Century. Mischel, an Austrian-American immigrant who arrived in America as a young boy, grew-up with an awareness that foreign-raised children seemed to have far better self-control than American-raised children. His curiosity brought him to design a study that examined how four- to six year-olds make decisions. When given the choice, would the children choose to have one marshmallow now (immediate gratification) or two marshmallows after a fifteen-minute wait (deferred gratification)?

Of the hundreds of children tested, only one-third were successfully able to defer gratification—to sacrifice a smaller payoff *now* for a bigger payoff in the *future*. However, the most interesting part of the story was yet to come. What Dr. Mischel would discover about those children, ten to twenty years later, is one of the most important lessons we can learn for college success.

Upon contacting the original subjects, now in their teens and twenties, Mischel discovered a telling correlation. The one-third of subjects who as children were able to delay their gratification for a bigger pay-off were faring much better than those who took the immediate gratification— those who couldn't wait. Not only were these individuals attending college and academically outperforming their cohorts, they were also enjoying more successful relationships and fewer interpersonal struggles.

In my years as a student and as a professor, I have noticed two general trends regarding culture and student performance. The majority of my students who grew up outside of America, as well as the majority of my older (non-traditional) students, tended to earn the highest grades. We know from research that the main factor in how someone comes to learn deferment of gratification–*self-discipline*–is through modeling from the parents, learned at an early age.

In other words, the thing that both of these groups have in common is that they were raised by parents who were born in different places and in different times than the majority of their classmates. Parents who were born just after World War Two, before the *now-on-credit* culture of instantaneous gratification became full-blown, raised the older students. The cultures outside of the US are more likely to have cash-based economies. Many students of both of these demographics were raised in an atmosphere of economic conscientiousness and savings for a future pay-off.

The American generations since the 1970s have been bred on a *"why wait?"* philosophy, and from credit cards to "one-click" shopping; most adults today are not very well exercised in delaying gratification.

Unfortunately many will never develop this skill that is necessary for academic and professional success. Many of the struggles of contemporary, American culture, from concentration problems to debt, are highly correlated with instantaneous gratification and the ability to endure the wait for the bigger pay-off.

So what is it that successful students are holding-off doing? What is the bigger pay-off? It can be as simple as staying in and working on a paper rather than going out to a party, with the foreknowledge that one day that sacrifice will pay-off, four-fold. Being able to set priorities and to put work before play goes a long way in college success.

Work and play: an exception to the rule

There is one quality that the most successful people share, and it requires a lot of play. These people *chose to do what they love*. The most celebrated geniuses of any time will tell you that they would do their work without pay if they could afford to. When you love what you are doing, it ceases to be work and becomes more like the childhood hours spent in play. When we do what we love, we do not become exhausted; instead we become invigorated and energized. The very act of our work gives us a sense of fulfillment and accomplishment. Ask those professors whom you find to be the most inspiring; they will tell you that they can't wait to get into the lecture hall every day. Do what you love and success will follow.

Scheduling reading, research, and study time

When you finally graduate from college you might not remember much of the information that you studied over the past four years. However, there is one thing you will know how to do like a professional: complete multiple projects at once.

In a given week you might be preparing for two exams, researching for a paper in one class, and writing a paper for another class. At times it feels so overwhelming that you might not know where to begin. The key to mastering this task is ORGANIZATION.

You will need some kind of schedule book. This can be on your phone, your laptop, or in an old-fashioned, paper and pencil planner. When you have a full course load with overlapping deadlines the last thing you want to encounter is a surprise. Here is a solid technique for you to stay completely organized and on top of your coursework.

The first day of class you are going to come home, sit down, and get out your syllabi for each class. Enter every exam, project, and topic date into your planner. You can color code by class with a colored pencil or even set unique alarm sounds on your phone for an exam, paper, or study session. The important thing is to make sure there are no surprises when it comes to your coursework.

Start by entering all of the exam dates, paper due dates, and project presentations. You will find that some of your weeks will be fairly sparse and then, *wham!*–a week full of tests. If you plan ahead you will be completely prepared to accomplish all of these obligations successfully. Remember, this is one of those habits, a secret, of the "A" students.

After you have entered each exam date, you will schedule study time for each exam. How much study time you will need varies by individual. I would plan on spending about two hours, per class, each day, for preparation. If you schedule two hours per day for each course, that will be about eight hours of study time per day. This is one reason why it is important to take fewer classes. Four classes is the limit I recommend for my student advisees. Five or six classes result in poorer grades and a lower GPA, not to mention stress, misery, and defeat. Occasionally I will encounter a student that can handle five or six classes, but it is extremely rare and often wishful thinking. Avoid setting yourself up for failure by taking on too many classes. Take as few as possible, and take them well. If you are the one out of ten students that can handle six courses, then disregard this message.

In your planner, schedule two hours per day for each class you are taking. It is important to also schedule time off. This can be one evening per week as well as daily, short, breaks. But remember the marshmallows: college is a brief few years that offers a greater payoff for the sacrifice and hard work.

After you have penciled-in two hours per day for each class, you can begin to enter the specific chapter readings and topics. You will have to judge for yourself how to allot your time. I would suggest breaking the reading up into smaller periods of time while taking short breaks. Because we each read and comprehend in different ways, it will be necessary for you to develop a reading schedule that is uniquely your own. Here are a few examples to help you.

I remember Maria, an undergraduate student who came to me for advice on how to study for an upper-level psychology course. Maria could manage small bursts of fifteen minutes of reading. After fifteen minutes she would stand up from her desk, walk around the room, and then return to her reading. She found that this method best suited her comprehension style (more about reading versus comprehending in Chapter 3). Maria was capable of reading about six pages in an hour, with thoughtful comprehension. Because the typical textbook chapter is around forty pages long, it took her about six hours (or three days) to read a chapter.

Maria knew her learning style and adjusted her schedule accordingly. When filling out her weekly schedule she marked page numbers by the day, covering the entire chapter in the first half of the week. On Thursday she would begin the next chapter on the syllabus. In this way, Maria was able to take small, bite-sized chunks of information and chew on them slowly—without choking. By taking in the information gradually we increase our ability to remember it for the future. But we will talk more on memorization in Chapter 6.

Another student, Shawn, had the enviable ability to read large amounts of difficult material, in a short period of time. Shawn's style of reading and comprehending required that he spend just one day with one or two chapters. Shawn's style is one in which the chapter is read, and retained, in one sitting. This manner is rare compared to most reading styles, and it leaves some of us wishing we could read that way. However, the thing to remember is that both approaches are *styles of reading* and require the organization and commitment to do the reading. Most students fail not because they don't understand, but because they do not plan-out and pace their reading.

The key here is to discover your own style of reading and then apply the formula repeatedly. For Maria, the formula was three days per chapter with frequent breaks. For Shawn it was one evening per chapter. Discover how you read and schedule your routine accordingly. The organization alone will improve your retention of the material, as well as improving your grades.

Where to study

Determining where you should study—in a softly lit quiet room, or a lively café—depends on the individual. Some folks study best, earbuds in, listening to Brahms while sitting in the local coffee shop, while others crave the silence of their private study. The best place for you to study is a very personal choice.

The goal is to discover where you do your best work. This takes some trial and error, but once you find your study spot, you will know it by the ease in which you are able to "sink" into the material.

I am a firm believer that one can learn to "sink" into single-minded concentration nearly anywhere and under almost any circumstances. But this takes practice.

Study partners and study groups

Psychologists have found evidence suggesting that our personality determines whether we choose to participate in group or individual sports. For some folks the idea of being part of a team means a loss of control over the outcome of the game and the frustration of having to work within a structure. For those who enjoy being part of a team, the idea of playing an individual sport, like tennis or running, is tedious and boring.

The same can be true for assignments and studying. Many of your classes will involve *group projects* in which you will be responsible for a component of the assignment.

Some love being a part of a group project and others loathe it. Taken on the whole, it is important to gain experience in working as a member of a group. Typically, even the most individualist student finds a rewarding experience—if paired with group members who complement one another's working style. And that is the important thing to remember about studying alone versus studying with a partner or a group—choose your buddies wisely.

I have always been an individual sports kind of guy. In college, and later at university, I came to abhor the group projects that were assigned in class. I strongly felt what the old saying "too many cooks spoil the soup" summed-up, that working with others diminished, rather than enhanced, my work. When it came to studying, I never studied in a group or with a partner. To be honest, the idea of studying with someone seems like a distraction to me. However, so many of my students have declared otherwise, claiming that group studying was one of the most beneficial things they did, that I have to reconsider my obstinate position.

Some of the students that celebrate group study tell me that it helped them to learn their own, individual, process of studying, assisted them in covering material that they otherwise would have overlooked, and even introduced them to new ideas and methods of studying. It's hard for me to argue against these points; I will let you determine for yourself.

Reading and marking the text

Over the years I have come to realize something very alarming about many college students—they don't know how to read! Now I am not talking here about reading in the literal sense, but of the ability to accurately comprehend what they read.

Sometimes students will come to my office to go over an exam that they had taken. I typically ask these students to read aloud the question that they answered incorrectly, so that we can both hear what is being asked. An amazing thing becomes apparent when some students read a question aloud: they are reading what they *think* the question is asking, rather than *what* the question actually asks. In fact, the answers that they are giving are often the correct answers, but to the wrong questions! Due to a variety of reasons, including nervousness and impatience, students often add, substitute, or miss entire words, altering the meaning of the question.

When we are reading, we have to slow down, commit ourselves to remaining in the now (not thinking about the party later, or the conversation earlier), and thoroughly read each sentence accurately. It does not matter how long you study something, if what you study has been misread the answer remains wrong.

Another common reading problem is how the student handles difficult or confusing sections. Sometimes it is tempting to skip past a puzzling sentence and move on to something that is not mystifying. This strategy is okay, as long as you mark the confusing section and return to it.

Sometimes we mark the section, intending to return to it, or ask the professor for clarification, but never follow though. These difficult concepts are the ones we later encounter on the exam. If you do not understand a passage, mark it, research it, and bring it up in class. Ignoring it is the worst thing to do.

This also holds true for vocabulary. I read with a dictionary at my side. I even have a dictionary application for my phone. I cannot imagine sitting down to read a college-level text without a dictionary, and neither should you. If you are skipping over a word because you don't understand it, you are cheating yourself and guaranteeing disaster on the next exam. You must get in the habit of looking-up unfamiliar words and writing the meanings in the margins of the book. This is like money in the bank.

There is one crippling habit you should break, if you have it. I'm referring here to the manic highlighting (or underlining) habit. If you find that after reading a page of text, more than one-third of the page is highlighted, you have a problem. I say highlighting, because it seems that students who are inclined to choose bright, florescent, highlighting markers tend to have this habit more than students who use a simple, understated pencil. I am not sure what it is about highlighting markers that turn a reader into a neurotic text marker, but the result is a messy hodgepodge of text and neon, which is probably contributing to confusion and interfering with memorization.

Listen: just because you have it highlighted does not mean that you know it! Somehow this whole highlighting craze seems to be related to territory marking, more than the demarcation of an important concept. It seems to be a habit of "Jerry (or Carol, Jim, Maria) was here!" Get away from these markers as soon as possible and get yourself a nice, dark, pencil.

Using a pencil allows you not only to underline salient passages, but also, to make comments within the margins. Since so many students seem to have trouble with this, I am going to describe my personal method for marking texts.

One of the most frustrating things about most college textbooks is that the coated, magazine grade paper that is used for printing makes a poor medium for pencil. You will find that making notes on the regular, cottony, paper of typical (not textbook) books, is much better for pencil marking. There is not much we can do about this magazine paper fad, other than wait for it to go away.

I always have my pencil at hand; in fact I keep about six of them strategically placed around the room, where I typically find myself needing a pencil. This is because when I read I walk around, going from seat to seat, which somehow helps me to think. Whenever I find a word that I am unfamiliar with I circle it, look it up, and then write a familiar synonym next to it.

When I come across a thought that I really agree with, I typically bracket it and write, "yes!" in the margin. If I disagree with the thought, I usually write "no!" (or some profanity) next to the bracketed segment. I will also write any thoughts that seem important in the margin next to the passage. My friends who later borrow my books enjoy my irreverent, marginal rants.

The only other mark that I make in my text is a "GQ" (signifying Golden Quote) next to any phrase that would be good to use in a paper. This has to be one of the best habits I have ever gotten myself into. When I am ready to write an essay, or book chapter, all I have to do is go back to the text and browse all of the juicy passages that I can add to my paper for emphasis and variety.

Choosing classes and choosing professors

Something that I hear from students on a regular basis, and a lesson that I remember learning in my first year of college, is: *the professor can make or break the class.* This lesson might not be as obvious is as it sounds, so let me explain.

A good teacher, those professors who not only hold our attention but also stay in our minds for the rest of our lives, seems to be able to make *any* topic interesting. I am saying this without apology–a teacher that not only knows the information, but also, knows *how to reach the students*, can successfully teach *anything*. The opposite is also true. Many "experts" in their field are incapable of explaining and *enchanting* students. This is important to keep in mind when you choose your classes.

Those professors that we talk about outside of class, and remember for the rest of our lives, are few and far between. In your years of college you might only encounter a handful that truly engage, move, inspire, and speak to you as if you were the only student in the class. Those professors quickly gain a reputation amongst students and colleagues, and rapidly become popular lecturers with packed classrooms. The professors who are not so engaging, who might "know their stuff" but remain aloof, distant, and uninspiring, often have empty seats and quiet office hours.

Seek out the captivating and inspiring professors and take as many as you can. Very often we fall in love with a subject through its presentation. A lifeless, disinterested, and uninspiring professor can make the most fascinating topic dull. If you get stuck with one of these professors, don't dismiss the subject—dismiss the professor!

So how do you know whom to take and whom to avoid? Stephanie, a junior in New York City, says, "Use the internet!" Today there are numerous professor-rating sites, and most professors maintain their own personal websites. When scheduling your classes, run the professors' name through the search engine then read, listen, and watch them in action! If you are lucky you will find audio and video of their lectures and interviews. Some professors maintain podcasts, blogs, and write for academic and commercial periodicals. Today it is easier than ever to checkout professors *before* enrolling in their class.

The traditional way to get the inside scoop on whom (and whom not) to take is by asking around. Ask upper classmates, advisors, and previous professors whom you have enjoyed. Ask "hey, whom do you recommend for this class?" Very often advisors know the insider information on whom students rave (and rant) about. Gather as much information as you possibly can about each professor to make sure that you are giving yourself the best experience available. Remember, fifteen weeks with the right professor can be life changing.

Another thing to consider is how to choose which classes to take. We have already discussed that a lighter course load is preferable to a heavier one, but even with that lighter course load there are some pitfalls to avoid when scheduling.

The first thing to consider when scheduling your classes is coursework balance. If, for instance, you are required to take a difficult physics module with lab, you probably want to balance that out with one or two courses in something different (*not* more math or science). Maybe this is the perfect time to fulfill that fine arts or health requirement? Some elective courses, such as yoga or meditation, can be the perfect complement to your physics and calculus requirements. Make sure that you save and use those electives wisely—they will be an oasis of joy during demanding semesters.

Remember that *when* you schedule your classes can mean everything. Those professors with the outstanding reputations end up with students on waiting lists, hopeful to get a seat. The more popular the professor, the quicker their classes close. Because of this it is imperative that you schedule the first day of registration. One student told me that she actually schedules her classes at the stroke of midnight on the day course registration opens, just to make sure that she gets to study with her first-choice professors. A little research and a little planning can go a long way!

3 HOW TO STUDY

"There is creative reading as well as creative writing."
                                        -Ralph Waldo Emerson

Guerrilla studying

I am a firm believer that learning and studying is an adventure and a passion, rather than a laborious duty. Like all fun things, it becomes laborious and dreadful when it is saddled with requirements that have little to do with learning, zeal, and exploration—namely exams. In a perfect world, everyone feels compelled to learn, without the threat of a poor grade, leaving no need for tests. Those who truly love to learn, study for the desire of wisdom, not from the fear of failure.

However, you are probably not in the utopian classroom, and you will have to study for an exam, rather than studying for the joy of learning. Just because you have to study in this way does not mean that studying must be painful. I have some recommendations on how to maximize your passion and enthusiasm, while minimizing your dread in studying. I call it "guerrilla studying."

In traditional study methods, the student is expected to use the textbook and notes as the main resources for study. Watching videos, listening to radio shows, and surfing the Internet was not part of "serious" study. However, going to the library to read books and journal articles was viewed as "legitimate" study. The traditional system privileged a certain kind of media—*print media*. Other forms of media were not considered to be a serious way to learn.

I reject the traditional model and propose that you undertake "guerrilla studying." Guerrilla studying is so effective that you will forget that you are studying. It simply replaces the drudgery of *study* with the enthusiasm of *discovery*!

You begin by taking the tried and true method of traditional study—you read the book and attend the lecture. But after that, it is a free-for-all of exploration. Begin by hitting the Internet. Put the topic of study into a search engine and see what you hit on. Read through the top five websites, see what Wikipedia says (yes, even Wikipedia is fair game in guerrilla studying), check out link 49 in the search results, look at the videos, and even check out the books on Amazon. The key here is to become completely immersed in the topic, and to use critical thinking to separate the wheat from the chaff.

Research has shown that exposure to the same information through different sources, increases learning, memorization, integration with previous information, and retention. Not to mention it is fun! If you are really adventurous you might try starting your own blog to share with others what you have found in your explorations. That is *guerrilla studying.*

Study to teach

When I was in college I knew that, one day, I was going to be a college professor. The goal was absolutely clear to me—I wanted to teach college students. Keeping that goal in mind, I considered every class I took to be an opportunity to learn something new *to teach*. When I was studying, in my mind, I was preparing to give a lecture, not to take an exam.

There is an old quip that to truly know something you have to be able to teach it. I think that applying this insight to studying is very useful. If you study and prepare for an exam as if you are going to be teaching the topic to a class, you will have become familiar with the material in a way that can only have positive consequences on test day.

How do you go about preparing for a lecture? You begin by reading, understanding, and committing to memory all of the salient information in the chapter. Although you cannot lecture on everything in the chapter, you must be able to field students' questions on everything in the text.

Once you have worked through all the text material, you research what other professors are teaching and how they are teaching it. I do this by watching and listening to recorded lectures that are available online by schools like MIT, the University of California at Berkeley, and Yale.

Once I have done all of this, I organize the information in my mind, sketch out a schematic that includes the most important aspects of the chapter, and finally rehearse my lecture by teaching it to an imaginary class. As an undergrad I even went as far as to write lecture notes, handouts, and create presentation slides! My desire was to know the material so well, that I would be able to teach it.

This method might not be for everyone, and it does demand a great deal of preparation. I present this to you more as a model for how you can go about motivating yourself to prepare as well as possible for the exam. Put your entire self into the preparation, and tap into the goals that matter most to you, as a method for motivation.

The 4-step "A-Effort" method for studying

When I was an undergraduate student studying for my psychology degree, I set out to develop a method of study that would practically ensure that I would get no less than a "B" on an exam. With the exception of one incident (a very bad math final in which my mind completely blanked), this method has worked without fail. I consistently earned high "A's" on all of my examinations and I learned the material so thoroughly that I still remember much of it to this day. This approach, which I call the *"A-Effort" study method*, is based on doing your best by thorough preparation and exhaustive mastery of the material. I encourage you to learn and to use this method at least once or twice. Ultimately you should develop a method of study that is tailored to your own personal strengths.

By the way, using the "A-Effort" method, I went into that math final with a 97% average, managing to get a "B+" in the course. It is always important to leave room for error.

The technique follows four basic steps:
1. Read the chapter
2. Read through the chapter making a flash card for each key concept
3. Memorize the flash cards for that chapter
4. Read the chapter one final time

Step 1: Read the chapter

Many of us have not developed the ability to comprehend and remember while we are reading. The act of reading itself, without contemplation and consideration, is like swallowing food without chewing. We have to chew and digest information, rather than merely consume it. This is a skill that some are taught at a young age, others figure out along the way, and some are now hearing for the first time. No matter which way, there are some effective ways of making the content of the chapter *meaningful*, which means you will be more likely to remember it.

When reading a chapter it is important to always ask yourself, "How does this relate to my life?" If your reaction to this question is something like "this has nothing to do with me," you have allowed your frustration to interfere with your ability to learn. You will have to *shift your attitude* to one that can find some relevance to your goals and life. The attitude that you choose to hold towards the material that you are studying will determine how well you digest and retain it for the examination. The task is to make it relevant to your life.

In some classes, like psychology or writing, the significance might be clear. In other courses it could be more challenging to see, but if you sincerely open your heart to *wanting* to learn the subject matter, you will greatly increase your chances of doing well in the course. The attitude with which you approach the material will greatly determine how well you learn it. Fostering the right attitude can be as simple as *finding personal relevance*, or imagining yourself as a *teacher preparing to lecture*.

Finding personal relevance means always asking the question *"How does this apply to my life?"* By making it personal—finding personal relevance to your life—you will increase the significance of the content thus making it more memorable. Researchers agree that personal relevance is one of the key factors in information retention.

Preparing to lecture is a technique in which you prepare the newly learned material with the goal of teaching others rather than being tested. Most educators agree that in order to teach another, one must truly master the material being taught. Use this to your advantage. Imagine you are going to be teaching the material that you are reading to the class. This will force you to be aware of salient points, to organize the material in a manageable way, and to present it in a way that will make it meaningful. Those who dream of one day becoming a teacher will find that developing this skill is essential. It is not uncommon in the first years of teaching to be only a few chapters ahead of your students when asked to teach an unfamiliar course within your area of study. Look at this as training on how to prepare to be a good teacher.

Reading a chapter for the first time should be an adventure in discovering new ideas. Do not attempt to retain every detail of the chapter; to do so is exhausting and useless. Simply sit back, get lost in the writing, and enjoy yourself! It is often helpful to make a note in the margin of the book or in a notebook, marking things that really strike you as interesting. Of course, the most interesting things we remember without trying. For classes in which a paper is required, it is helpful to mark good quotes as you come across them. I am in the habit of bracketing and marking "GQ" (golden quote) in the books that I am reading. This will make excellent material for essay assignments as well as professional writing that you might undertake.

Step 2: Making flash cards

If you really want to waste your time, make big, detailed, longwinded flash cards with verbatim definitions. I can think of no greater waste of energy and useless activity. The thing that makes information *stick* is the intention, the act of putting something into your own words. Lose the big, wordy, definitions that you are given in the textbook and instead chew and digest *the idea* until you can express it in your own words. Emerson teaches us that "genius is the ability to express complicated ideas in the simplest ways," and I agree. If you can take an advanced concept and explain it to a middle-schooler, you know it!

I prepare my 3X5" note cards by cutting them in half. This makes them easy to put in my pocket, reduces how much I can write, and cuts the cost in half! As I read the chapter for the second time, I carefully make a flash card for each key concept in the chapter.

Today, most college textbooks list the important words in the margins or print them in bold font. Pause at each word, put the definition in your own words, and make the flash card. As research shows, we often remember visually, so don't hesitate to make your definition in the form of a picture. The key is to make it condensed—brief and full of punch!

When you have completed reading the chapter for the second time you should have a stack of about thirty or forty, small, square, flash cards that will easily fit into your pocket.

Step 3: Memorizing the flash cards

This step requires that you follow my instructions carefully. I have developed this technique to incorporate nearly every aspect of effective memorization: *organization, visualization, chunking, relevance, time, and repetition*. The first rule is to always keep the flash cards in the order in which they were made, chronologically with the text. Flash cards at the top of the stack will have occurred earliest in the chapter. As you prepare new chapters it is also important that you keep each chapter in separate stacks, labeled and secured by a rubber band.

Now you have about forty flash cards that represent the chapter you are preparing to be tested on. Take the top three flash cards from the stack and place the remainder in your left pocket. Keeping the three flash cards in order, memorize them until you can think the definition without pause. Because you have made the flash cards in a manageable size, you can discretely study them while walking down the street, on the bus or subway, or between classes.

When you have mastered the first three cards, place them in your right pocket (the *learned* stack) and take the next three from the left, *unlearned*, stack. Memorize these three new, flash cards until they are second nature. This should take about ten minutes.

Next, being careful to maintain the original order of the cards, combine the first three flash cards with the second three, resulting in six flash cards.

You will find that it will take a few minutes to integrate the six cards into memory. When you are able to rapidly and accurately think of the definitions for all six cards, return them to the *learned* pocket and take three more *unlearned* cards. Repeat this until all of the cards from the left pocket have made their way to the right pocket.

By the end of the week you will have memorized the key concepts so well that you will be able to revisit them only twice a day (once in the morning and once at night) in order to maintain them. By this time you will be able to move on to the next chapter and repeat the sequence of reading, making flash cards, and memorizing.

Step 4: Final reading

At the end of three weeks you will have three memorized stacks of flash cards (one for each chapter) and have read each chapter twice. To seal the deal, sit down and read through each chapter. You will find that you are so well prepared for the examination that it is unlikely to score lower than an "A." Of course, test taking is another issue, and regardless of how well you have prepared, if you do not know *how to take a test* you will not do your best.

4 HOW TO TAKE EXAMS

"The reward of a thing well done is having done it."
-Ralph Waldo Emerson

I want to make something perfectly clear before discussing test taking with you. This is something that I want you to remember for the rest of your college career, and for you to pass on to your children when they are of school age. *Tests reflect less on what you know, and more on how skilled you are at taking tests.* I am telling you this not only as a professor, but also as a psychologist. Tests are a measure of test-taking ability.

My earliest education was in a Montessori school. I later attended a parochial Catholic school, went on to a public high school, and then on to an American college and a European graduate school. When it comes to education systems, I have experienced a variety. Each of these systems was unique in how it assessed understanding, and I think that describing them to you will make you a better exam taker.

Entering into a parochial, Catholic school was a culture shock after attending Montessori school. The contrast was extreme and, in my experience, could not have been more different. Whereas Montessori school nurtured the skills of individual exploration and how to figure things out on your own, Catholic school taught us what to think and when to think it. The shift from one of the most humanistic and liberal education models to one of the most conservative and dogmatic was a transition that really brought to my attention that *how* something is taught and *how* students are regarded greatly determines *how* that student will come to regard learning.

The transition from Catholic school to public school taught me something else about learning. I had gone from a culturally homogenous class of ten students, to a economically diverse classroom of thirty plus students. I didn't quite understand it at the time but, looking back, there was a social and class tension that existed in public school that was not so apparent in the private schools that I had attended previously. I think that this was the first encounter with the social distinction that I would come to know as *haves* and *have-nots*.

In Catholic school everyone dressed in the same uniform, so it was less apparent that we may not all be coming from the same socioeconomic backgrounds. Although, I suspect, we all did.

The Montessori school students all had at least one thing in common—extremely progressive parents who sought out experimental education. But in public school it was different.

If Montessori school was all about exploring and Catholic school about self-discipline, then public school was about maintaining order and managing a classroom full of disparate students from various backgrounds. In my memory, the public school teacher's priority was maintaining order.

Along with those large classes came another new experience—how we were assessed. In Montessori school there were no "tests" per se. And in Catholic school exams were typically written essays and recitation, not unlike what I would later encounter in European university. The main way a professor assessed your knowledge was through papers and discussions. The "objective" test, which I encountered for the first time in public school, was something that the teachers used out of practicality because there were so many students to grade.

I was not tested in my university education. I was assessed through written essays, oral defense, and classroom discussion (save a one-year period where I studied psychology in a state university). I did not have "objective" *multiple choice* or *true-false* exams after my public school days.

It is my opinion that the best way to evaluate a students' knowledge is through their written and oral delivery of that knowledge. Things we learn in class rely on communication, as do our personal and professional lives. "Objective" tests that rob students of the ability to express their knowledge individually and elaborately remain necessary as long as we have factory-schools that mass-produce graduates.

Today, even in the smallest and most elite colleges, you will need to know how to take not only essay and oral exams, but also, multiple choice and true-false exams. Fortunately, there are some methods that you can use to beat the "objective" test machine.

Don't let the test take you

Here is my number one piece of advice to you. For any kind of examination, whether it is in essay, oral, or multiple-choice format: *You take the test, don't let the test take you!* Be like the samurai who focuses on "meeting the other sword," not desiring to conquer the opponent or to cut him. The samurai master completely focuses on the joy of the movement of the swords. The master overcomes (*masters*) the desire to conquer. The master samurai's actions are a poetic act of control, rather than a frantic grasping for survival and triumph.

You must emulate the samurai when *you take the test*. It is *you* who are in control of the exam, not the exam that is in control of you. This simple shifting of perspective can change your test-taking life forever.

When I coach students in test taking they typically chuckle at the image of a test-taking samurai. But I tell you, that is the attitude you must acquire to master the test: quiet, calm, and poetically deliberate with every answer. This is an attitude that requires cultivation and practice. Here is how you can start.

Going within

To do your best on an exam, you must cultivate the ability to turn off the outside world and to tune in to your internal world. If you are able to remain fully absorbed in your own, self-directed, intentional thoughts about the topic, you will achieve your *master* potential at test taking. The ability to completely lose oneself in one's own world, to wholly eliminate both external and internal distractions is not accomplished immediately. It is a skill that must be learned and practiced daily.

If you have not learned meditation, I suggest you begin now. Meditation is the single most important skill you can learn to be a better exam taker. Meditation is different than relaxation techniques in that meditation is about complete psychological control of that which is usually on "autopilot." I am talking here about the experience of distraction, nervousness, negative self-talk, and damaging negative emotions. All of these things seem uncontrollable, but they are not. You can learn through meditation how to take control of those seemingly automatic responses that derail your ability to take the exam.

There are many styles of meditation and many methods. You should explore the various traditions and chose one that is most suited to your worldview and which works best. I am going to teach you a basic meditation technique that will serve as a first step towards adopting a method of your own.

This meditation technique comes from the Buddhist tradition and focuses on mind training. It is a technique that exercises your ability to *stop the act of thinking* and gives your mind a rest. Actually, it is less about stopping thought and more about *focusing* thought. If you practice this meditation exercise for only ten minutes a day, every day, you will see an improvement in your concentration within a week's time. Here is how you do it.

You first must decide on a ten-minute period of time, every day, which you will not be disturbed. This might mean hiding from your friends and family in the bathroom, going to the library, bookstore, or park, or creating a special, *you-only* meditation space. Wherever you decide to meditate, make sure that you will be left in stillness to meditate for ten minutes. If this sounds unreasonable or impractical to you, you need to explore setting boundaries with the people in your life!

I meditate before going to bed. I find that meditating before bed ushers me into the most restful and rejuvenating sleep that I can achieve. Some folks like to meditate in the morning, to start their day focused, or even in the afternoon. Another option is to meditate at designated, multiple times throughout the day. I like to meditate once per day, and then as needed.

You begin by sitting or lying in a comfortable position. For this technique there is no special sitting position, just a naturally comfortable stance that allows you to feel secure, safe, and at-ease.

Next, close your eyes and look into the blackness. I am not kidding; look into your closed eyelids and wait. Within a few seconds you will begin to see patterns of light swirling and bursting in chaos. Scientists call these patterns *phosphenes*, and they are a product of our nervous system.

Watch these phosphene patterns, and enjoy them! Don't get caught-up in trying to determine what they look like, or what they are; just watch them and enjoy their dance –*your* neurological dance! Do this for ten minutes, allowing yourself to become completely engrossed by the neural lights.

Most people are not able to allow themselves to become completely absorbed with their phosphenes for ten minutes. The distraction that most people report is usually to internal, rather than external stimuli (chatter). The biggest difficulty in meditation is to remain in the experience, simply watching the patterns, without thinking about them. Not getting sucked into the anxiety producing *future*, or the emotionally burdensome *past*, remaining engaged within the *now* is to master meditation.

Begin by meditating every day for ten minutes. You can use your phone's timer or download a special meditation app. It takes most folks a few weeks before they experience their first ten-minute session of letting-go. After that initial experience, you will encounter it more and more frequently, until you are able to remain in the meditative state at will.

What's happening when you meditate is similar to the modern practice of *biofeedback*. In biofeedback you are learning to control breathing rate, heart rate, and mental content through manipulating an auditory or visual feedback cue. The automatic functions of heart rate, respiration rate, body temperature, and hormonal release, are all part of the *autonomic nervous system*. We never have to consciously remind ourselves to breathe or to beat our heart, it happens automatically, without conscious, deliberate control.

Meditation, like biofeedback, teaches us how to take conscious control of our autonomic functions, allowing ourselves to slow our heart, respiration, and automatic thinking, at our own discretion and will. Imagine having the ability to turn off your anxiety, nervousness, and stress, with a thought. That is exactly what the practice of meditation will bring to you.

This is not a "might bring you," or "maybe you can achieve it"; this is an absolute certainty that with persistence and practice you can learn how to do this. There is nothing mystical or supernatural about it. It is a simple, biological mechanism that you can learn to control. The problem is that we are typically never taught this skill in childhood.

Once you have practiced meditation for a few weeks, and have been able to allow yourself to stop thinking, you will have a powerful tool for test taking, public speaking, or any situation in which calm, deliberate, composure will benefit you. When faced with the situation, you simply think about your meditation and a calm, streaming energy will come over you. You literally need to train your body to do and to experience this sensation. Once you have, you will be the master of most of the circumstances you find yourself in.

Here is how I use meditation when taking exams. Before starting an exam I put down my pencil, lay my hands on my lap, and close my eyes. I bring about the calm that I have practiced on a daily basis and, when I am ready, I open my eyes. Conjuring up this calm, and picking up the pencil to begin—*when I am a ready*—is the key. *This is my declaration to myself. "I am taking this test; this test is not taking me."*

Once I begin, I remain aware of when I start to feel anxious, nervous, or when the test is "taking me." When I feel anxious I stop, put down my pencil, and close my eyes. Once the calm has resumed, I begin again. I pause and close my eyes as often as I need to, and I don't apologize for doing so.

The more you practice this technique and the more experience you get with actually implementing it, the more effective and efficient you will become in doing it. I am now at a point in which I can remain in the state of calm throughout an entire examination or presentation. But it took years of practice.

There are some additional things that you can do to enhance your ability for going within yourself while taking an exam. Here are a few of the things that I find useful when exam time comes.

When I take an exam I want to feel safe, anonymous, and alone. I find a place in the classroom to sit where I feel these things. Of course this means arriving to the room early enough to choose my seat. Some students like to sit close to the door, where they gain the sense that they can escape at any time. I like to sit in the back of the room, with my back to the wall. Wherever you feel safest, that is where you should sit on exam day.

I like to wear earplugs when I am taking an exam. Earplugs will keep the sighs, cries, and coughs of others out of your ears, and allow you to feel alone with yourself. In fact, I carry earplugs in my backpack, so that I can control silence whenever and wherever I choose. Try wearing earplugs during your next exam. Once you do, you will never go without!

Take the test twice

One of the biggest mistakes that students make is worrying about when other students finish the exam. They see some eager student hand in his or her test and think to themselves, "Wow, they must have really studied."

I have been grading exams for ten years and I can tell you this for certain: student who hands their exam in twenty minutes before the other students begin trickling up usually failed the exam. Whereas the perception is that the students really knew their stuff and did well, the truth is that they didn't know their stuff and bailed out as soon as possible. They simply got it over with. Don't be fooled by those students who complete an exam in record time—they are often lucky if they passed with a "D."

On the other end of the spectrum are the students who are still going over their answers, long after the majority of the class has gone home. These students typically do much better on the exam than the other students. Because they are going over the questions and their answers a second time, double-checking for accuracy, they are taking more time with the test. I watch these students in action. They complete the exam. Stop for a moment. Take a breath, and then retake the exam, making sure that they read each question accurately, while confirming their answer. The students who take the test twice, before submitting, are the ones who are earning the "A's." I will put my money on that statement.

In fact, double-checking your exam is so essential that I am going to repeat it and drive it home with an example. If you are not taking your exam twice before handing it in, you are cheating yourself out of the best possible grade that you could be getting. This, by far, is the one piece of advice that has made the most difference in my students' grades. Double-check your answers before submitting the test.

Of course, most of us want to take the exam and get it over with as quickly as possible. The exam time is stressful and nerve-racking, and it can feel intolerable while we are in it. The relief of just getting it over with is sometimes a more promising pay-off than making more sweat by going over the test a second time. I promise you this, and you can write me hate mail if I am wrong, if you take the time to retake the test before you submit it, your grade will improve by at least one letter grade.

Multiple-choice questions

When it comes to multiple-choice questions, it is mostly about test-taking skills and least about knowledge. Let me convince you of this. I asked forty of my best students to return to campus after the semester had been completed to take a test. These students had all earned high "A's" in my Introduction to Psychology course and were screened to determine their knowledge and experience in the field of media studies. I then administered a standard, multiple-choice exam on the topic that none of them had studied—media theory. The results were astounding: not one of the students failed the exam, and most of the students earned a "C" or better.

These results convinced me of my long-held belief that multiple-choice tests require test-taking skills, and these students had developed those skills.

Over the past ten years I have read many books and explored many websites that offer advice on multiple-choice test taking. There are so many resources available for this information that it is curious that many students come into the college classroom completely unfamiliar with them. Well, here is a compilation of those techniques that I have found to be the most effective.

When taking any test, but particularly when dealing with multiple-choice items, make sure that you read the instructions carefully. Most multiple-choice instructions ask you to "choose the best answer." Look at these words again, slowly. What is it telling you to do? I can tell you what most students *think* that it is instructing—*and they are wrong*. Most students interpret these words as meaning "choose the correct answer."

If you are looking for the one, correct, answer out of four choices, you are setting yourself up for failure. Why? Because when most professors write their questions they include more than one correct answer. Most students get a question wrong not by answering incorrectly, but by not choosing the *best* answer—*the answer that is more correct than the others.* Typically the professor will lead-in to the correct answer, building up to it. If you find the correct answer and feel that you do not have to read the remaining choices, you are increasing your chances of getting it wrong. Don't be cock-sure on this! Read all of the answers. Chances are that you are going to discover an even better answer deeper in the choices. If rule number one is read the instructions, then rule number two is read all of the answers before selecting the *best* one.

I advise my students to take the entire multiple-choice exam, answering as best they can, and skipping the questions that confuse them. I tell them to circle these baffling questions and put them aside for phase-two of the test taking process, which is going back to the difficult questions.

Phase one: answer all of the questions that you know. *Phase two:* answer the questions that you do not know. *Phase three:* take the test again, making sure that you did not misread or *mis-answer* a question.

Very often it is possible to find the answers to difficult questions in the exam itself. It is nearly impossible for a professor to ask one question without providing the answer, or at least a big clue, to another question. By skipping the difficult questions until after you have read through the entire test, you are increasing your chances of finding the correct answer hiding somewhere in another question. You will do much better answering the difficult questions after reading the entire exam, rather than just cold guessing to get it over with.

When answering a question, I read it thoroughly. I will read it a few times to make sure that I really understand what it is asking. I typically spend a few minutes on each question. Before reading the answers, I try to think of what the correct answer might be. I then carefully read through all four options. If I find an answer that is close to the one I had imagined, I put a star next to it.

Next, I look for the answers that I know are dead wrong. Typically there is an answer that is wrong but related to the question, and an answer that is wrong and completely unrelated to the question. There is also a good answer, and a really good answer. Here are some typical qualities of wrong answers. Don't choose them.

You can sometimes eliminate answers because they are grammatically incompatible with the question. If you read the answer and it doesn't fit grammatically, do not choose it. No professor will make a grammatically incorrect answer the correct answer.

Another sign of a blatantly incorrect answer is if it contains one of these words: *always, never, all, or none.* Nothing in life fits these absolute categories, and choosing answer with one of these words is *usually not* a good idea!

Sometimes you will be asked to choose a numeric amount, such as a percentage. A good rule of thumb for getting these questions correct is to always avoid extreme numbers. If you are choosing the lowest or the highest number from the four choices, you are decreasing you chances of choosing the correct answer. Most professors will frame the correct answer with numbers that are far too high or far too low.

You want to locate the "really good" (best) answer! To do this, cross out the two wrong answers. Find them, and literally put a line through them. Now you have increased your chances from 25% to 50% for answering correctly.

Now comes the difficult part, find which of the remaining two answers is more accurate, gives more detail, or more fully answers the question. If you can find that answer, you will have a good chance of being correct. Once you have gone through the entire test like this, return to answer those questions that were confusing.

Finally, go back and take the exam a second time. If you find yourself disagreeing with your first answer, spend some time understanding why. Did some other question make your answer incongruent with another question on the test? Was there some question that jostled your memory of a better answer? Make sure that you know *why* you are choosing to change your answer. Once you have gone through these three phases, you will have truly given an "A-Effort" in test taking.

True false questions

Although many college professors do not use true-false items on exams, they are common enough that a few pointers won't hurt. Let's begin with the nature of true-false questions. This type of question has no nuance, no ambiguity, and offers you a 50% chance at being right. The key to getting true-false items correct is careful reading.

Some students think that if a true-false statement is *mostly true,* or *more true than false*, then it is *true*. No. If there is *anything* about the statement that is false, or incongruent with other information within the statement, then it is a false statement. It does not matter if it is *almost completely true*, or 99.9% true, if it has even the slightest inaccuracy, then it is false. Read the statement, pause, and then read it again. If the statement is not entirely true, then it is false.

In true-false statements, like multiple-choice questions, qualifying words like: *sometimes, often, frequently,* or *ordinarily* are indicative of a true statement, whereas words like *always, never, all* and *none* indicate a false answer. Broadly sweeping generalizations are typically false.

Once I had a biology professor who made extremely difficult exams. I can honestly say that his exams were the most difficult objective tests I have ever taken. After failing the first exam, I promised myself a beautiful Swiss Army watch, if I completed the course with an "A".

I knew that I had to pull out all of the stops with this professor's exams. So I did what any self-respecting psychologist would do—I analyzed the first exam to find trends in his test construction. What I found was remarkable. So good, in fact, that other students paid me to teach them the trick of mastering this professor's tests. As far as I know, this technique still works with this professor's tests. Here it is for you.

I sat down and analyzed each true false and multiple-choice item. I found that 80% of the time this professor's true-false items were true. Nearly 70% of the time the correct multiple-choice answer was "C". This meant that regardless of the question, if I simply answered "C" for each multiple choice question, and true for each true-false question, I should get a "B" on the exam. I didn't try that theory out, but when completely baffled by a question, I knew how to choose an answer that increased my chances of being correct. By the way, if you ever run into me on the street, ask to see my Swiss Army watch!

Essay and oral exams

It has been my experience that the essay exam is, by far, the best format for testing students. The essay not only allows the student to express the areas of knowledge they have learned, it helps them to formulate that new information into a declared integration with other material. What does this mean for you, as a student? It means that an essay exam gives you a chance to really show what you know, and on your terms.

There are some good habits to follow when writing an essay answer. Grammar, spelling, structure and style are absolutely necessary, despite what your professor tells you.

Always pay close attention and proofread your answer before handing in the exam.

I like to think of the essay exam as a short paper. In this way, much of the advice that I offer in the chapter on paper writing holds true for the essay exam, only in briefer form. Whereas the typical paper ought to be no less than five pages, the standard essay should be no more than five paragraphs.

I organize my essay answers in *French dissertation style*, meaning, in three sections. The first section gives a brief background to the question being asked. The second section explores a specific aspect of that background, and the third section gives your position on the topic.

You can also think of this in terms of the three sections in which classical symphonies or sonatas are written. In classical music the three sections are called the *exposition* (tells what you are talking about), the *development* (goes into detail about what you are talking about), and the *recapitulation* (wraps up by integrating the first and second sections together).

A final analogy is called the *dialectic*, described by German thinker G.W.F. Hegel. The *dialectical method* describes the three sections as the: *thesis*, *antithesis*, and *synthesis*. The *thesis* presents the most prominent point of view. The *antithesis* describes a point of view that challenges the commonly held point of view. The *synthesis* brings the thesis and antithesis together to form a new idea.

Each of these variations, when used, will serve as a classic outline for writing outstanding essay answers. Utilizing the format itself should not only help you to organize your answer, but will also leave the reader (your professor) with the impression of a well-planned and executed essay.

I think of the oral exam as a spoken essay. In fact, you can prepare for an oral exam by writing an essay and using it as a script. Although oral exams are far less common today, you will encounter them in graduate school.

Test taking anxiety

Anxiety is what we experience when we are trying to control the future. In the case of test taking anxiety, we are attempting to control the outcome of our test. This feeling of heightened physical and emotional symptoms interferes with our performance and can actually lead to poor test grades. There are a few general rules to follow if you experience test-taking anxiety.

When we experience anxiety, our autonomic nervous system is preparing for survival in the event of potential conflict. For us, the conflict is the outcome of our performance on an exam. Although anxiety can be a great motivator to study for an exam, it does not seem to be of much benefit to us while taking an exam. To the contrary, it actually interferes with our performance.

If you experience test taking anxiety there are a few changes that you should make to reduce the symptoms. First and foremost, you need to begin training your physical and emotional reactions through meditation (described above). You should also avoid all stimulants, including nicotine, caffeine, and sugar. If you have anxiety problems, taking stimulants will make things worse.

Very often taking a non-caffeinated, herbal tea, or herbal supplement can be helpful in controlling anxiety. You can consult your physician or research anti-anxiety herbs in the library. I would like to talk, more specifically, about the psychological methods for controlling anxiety.

Anxiety is experienced when we face potential loss of control over a situation that threatens to have consequences on our well-being. Whether a car has just run a red light and we slam on the brakes, or a crucial exam is in our future, the emotional response is often a feeling of anxiety. For some students this anxiety is so severe that it incapacitates, or severely interferes, with their ability to take the exam to the best of their ability.

The best way to eliminate the fear of the loss of control is to gain a sense of control. Because the test taking experience is not totally in your control (your professor's test writing style and ability has a lot to do with it), you will need to give up a desire for *complete* control in order to gain a *sense of control.* This is a classic lesson of psychology given to us by philosopher Reinhold Neibhur—"God, give us grace to accept with serenity the things that cannot be changed, courage to change the things which should be changed, and the wisdom to distinguish one from the other."

What this means is that there are some things we can control and some things we can't control. If we have done our best at directing the things we *can* control, then we have done the best we can do. The rest is, literally, out of our hands. The task here is to know what you can control and what you cannot.

The next step in establishing and maintaining a sense of control is preparation. If you have prepared to the best of your ability and accepted that the outcome of the exam is only partly in your hands, you will feel a significant reduction in anxiety.

What does it mean to be well prepared? For starters it means following the suggestions in this book. It also means going above and beyond to get ready for the event of taking the test. In other words, practice taking tests. Ask your professor for practice questions, take the practice exams that are in most textbooks, and utilize the publisher's website (which often provides practice tests). The more exams you take, the more confident and comfortable you will become while taking an exam.

Sometimes we are our own worst enemy. We can be so hypercritical of ourselves that we barely stand a chance at feeling anything but dread and anxiety about our ability to handle what comes our way. How this internal finger wagging comes to be is debated by psychologists, but one thing is clear: we have a tendency to sabotage our performance with disapproving beliefs, judgments, and thoughts. Here are a few self-judgments that are common to those who experience test-taking anxiety, and some strategies for overcoming them.

One of the most common irrational beliefs is apparent in statements like "I have to get an 'A' or I'm a failure" or "If I don't graduate with honors I am worthless." Yikes! That is called *catastrophizing* and it is the king of irrational beliefs. The *good life* is made up of more than outstanding grades. The belief that *you are your grade* will bring you nothing but unhappiness. To think that anything less than an "A" is failing is just plain absurd. In fact, that kind of thinking has a name of its own: *all or nothing thinking.*

All or nothing thinkers have a tendency to view the world in either-or terms, often to their disadvantage. If you feel that you *must* earn an "A" on every test, you are not being reasonable with yourself and you have established the groundwork for a very exhausting life, one in which you will seldom feel contented.

Some of us amplify our failures and weaknesses while dismissing our triumphs and accomplishments. Somehow that one exam that we *bombed* takes the spotlight in our minds over the many that we mastered. If you only recall the bad moments of test taking, you are *filtering* out the good moments and creating an irrational belief that incubates anxiety. Stop dwelling on the negative!

Yet another debilitating belief is that if we work hard we will get the "A." Not true. Sometimes, no, as a rule, in life our greatest efforts do not dictate the outcome. Hard work does not guarantee that you will get an "A," but no work *will* guarantee failure. If you believe that an "A-effort" guarantees an "A" grade, you need to change your belief to fit the real world. The secret to success is satisfaction based on effort, not on the result.

5 HOW TO WRITE AN ACADEMIC PAPER

"It is a fact often observed,
that men have written good verses
under the inspiration of passion,
who cannot write well under other circumstances."

-Ralph Waldo Emerson

There is nothing that scares the college student more than freedom. I mean it terrifies them. Tell a student to write a paper on some exact topic or person and they are fine. Give them the liberty of choosing a topic and expressing their thoughts on it and they become dumbfounded and confused. Most students are masters at telling the professor what others think, dutifully footnoting some authority. When it comes to developing their own sense of authority, I have found that students are terrified to express themselves.

I think the reason for this is the current trend of teaching *facts* established by *authorities*, rather than *arguments* made by *thinkers*. I am encouraging you to be a *thinker*, rather than a *knower*.

Thinkers write their papers differently than *Knowers*. Both will always use the third person when writing an academic essay, avoiding the first person "I." Both will also give thorough background information and reference each quote and idea. However, thinkers do not stop there; they continue on to synthesize the ideas and present something innovative—an idea of their own. In addition to quoting the authorities, these writers learn to trust their ideas and themselves.

In this chapter I will teach you how to write like a *thinker* rather than a *knower*, and convince you that how you write will influence how you understand the world.

Mechanics

Before I tell you the juicy hints, let's get this out of the way. Always, without exception, have your paper proofread by a professional writer before submitting it. Every college employs a staff of writing experts that will proofread your papers, making them close to perfect. All it takes is a little planning and effort to deliver the paper to them. Even if you are told that spelling and grammar will not count, have your papers professionally edited, as a matter of self-respect. Remember to always be able to forgive yourself after an "A-effort," regardless of mistakes. Even after the most exhaustive proofing, errors will slip through. The goal here is conscientiousness, not compulsive perfection.

Finding your voice

How you write (your style) will be greatly influenced by what you read. If you do not read, you will have a difficult time learning how to write well. I recommend that you find an author whose style you really enjoy reading. Take the time to study this author's writing as frequently as possible, paying attention to what it is that makes their manner appealing to you.

I also encourage you to follow the advice of Hunter S. Thompson, who taught young writers to hand copy the works of their favorite authors to get their tempo, rhythm, and sentence structure into their fingers. Thompson claimed that if you did this, you would *feel* what it is like write well.

Imagine your audience

One of the best writing exercises I have ever done is rewriting the same essay three times, each time with a different audience in mind. Although the topic and information remains consistent, the style and format of the paper will change dramatically. Who do you write to in your papers?

Most students, when asked, tell me that they are writing to their professor. Sounds logical, but that approach might be hurting them. You see, when we write to someone whom we think knows more about the topic than we do, we have a tendency to leave out details and examples, assuming that the reader (the professor) already knows what we are writing about. To the professor's eyes, it seems that you have left out important information, and that maybe you need to do more research.

Do not write to your professor. Instead imagine some audience who knows little about the topic, and is relying on you to explain it. If you write your paper to someone who is intelligent, but knows little to nothing about the topic, you will necessarily write a more detailed paper, increasing your grade.

French Dissertation Style

When I arrived to study music at the Royal Conservatory in Brussels, some fifteen years ago, I was notified that I was required to take an academic course in world cultures. This would be my first academic classroom experience in Europe. Something that struck me was the way in which students answered the professor's questions. At the time I assumed that it was simply part of the "old world" style of the European conservatory (I had been told that in some universities it was still customary for the students to rise to answer). In time I came to adopt this style, which I learned not formally, but rather as an attempt to fit in.

It was not until years later, while studying towards my doctorate in Switzerland, that I learned that this way of answering was, in fact, a highly structured and formulaic, European tradition. It was introduced to me as the "French dissertation style."

When answering a question in the traditional French classroom (I understand that this is true at both school and university), one answers in three distinct parts. The first segment states the question and offers a brief history and contextualization of the question. The second focuses, in more detail, on one aspect of the historical contextualization of the question. The final, third part, allows the student to put forth their thought and argument about the question.

I distinctly recall the impression that it made years later when I answered questions this way in the American classroom. Most students and professors were not accustomed to the format and comprehensiveness of this answering style. It made a positive impression. I also found that my writing began to change. When given an essay in the class, I was disposed to write in the tertiary form (broad history, focus on one historical argument, and give my argument).

When I began teaching I decided to familiarize my students with this style. The result was spectacular. Students not only improved their essay writing, but also found that the format afforded them an advantage in other classes. With satisfaction and self-confidence, students proudly reported the reactions from classmates and professors to their thorough, "French" style. They also found that their essay grades increased, because answering (orally or written) in this way requires not only a very accurate understanding, but also a hesitation in giving one's opinion. One student likened it to proving that you had the right to make the argument, that you had "done your homework". I agree.

In preparing to teach this to my students, I did some formal research into the *French dissertation style*. I would like to share these formal guidelines with you, too.

The written aspect of the dissertation style is somewhat different from the oral response structure that I experienced in Belgium. The three-part format follows a Hegelian *Thesis-Antithesis-Synthesis* format.

The problem or question (the French call this the *problématique*) is stated. One can state the question in one of three different styles: *thematic type*, *interrogative type*, or *implicit subject type*. I have always liked the implicit subject type best because one can explore paradoxical connections that are typically unnoticed.

The next part is the presentation of the thesis or argument. Typically the line of reasoning is supported by three examples. An opposing argument or *antithesis* is then presented with supporting examples. Finally, the *synthesis* or presentation of the new idea (birthed from the *thesis* and *antithesis)* is given. This is where one gets to state their own ideas.

Lastly, an *introduction* (say what you are going to say) and a *conclusion* (say what you've said) are written. I have always told students that the *introduction* and *conclusion* should be the final things written—how could you know what you are going to say before you've said it (before writing it through)?

The written dissertation can be as brief as five paragraphs (one paragraph for each: the introduction, thesis, antithesis, synthesis, and conclusion) or book-length.

6 MEMORIZATION

My father is a great lover of the out-of-doors. Regardless of the season, or the weather, my father takes every opportunity to walk through the woods and enjoy nature. Typically my dad walks either with his four-legged companion, alone, or with me. When I accompany him on his walks, along the Blue Mountain of Pennsylvania, I get a glimpse inside my father's mind, because he starts to think aloud.

One afternoon, as we walked through the woods along an abandoned railroad bed, my father told me that the mind was like earth, and experiences like creeks and rivers. "Sometimes," he told me; "life comes all at once, like a big burst of water. That's when deep gorges are cut into the land." He described how the water sometimes passes thorough in one, immense episode, and having passed into the earth, leaves behind a residual gulley. "This," he told me, "is like a bad experience, one that leaves its mark on our minds." "Sometimes," he continued, "water runs slowly and continuously over the same ground, gradually forming a canal—like a small stream." This was the first time that I really appreciated that my father was a sage of nature.

My father's intuitive ideas about experience and memory have been more useful and profound to me than most of the experimental, academic theories that I have studied. However, his insights on memory do resonate with the work of two psychologists: Fergus Craik and Robert Lockhart.

Overshadowed by the older and popularized, *Atkinson and Schiffrin Model of Memory* (which described sensory, short-term, and long-term memory banks), Craik and Lockhart's *Levels of Processing Theory* is more in-line with my father's insights into memory. It is also the model that I have come to find most useful in teaching students how to memorize information. Let me explain.

There are some things that we remember without even trying. Certain thoughts, emotions, events, people, and observations seem to just stick with us. In therapy people are sometimes trying to deal with a memory that won't go away—we call it *trauma*. Trauma is like that big, sudden, unexpected burst of water that forever changes the landscape of the earth. It seems that trauma (unexpected, life-threatening events) often leaves a permanent trace in our minds.

Another thing that seems to stick with us is more positive events, like our first love, our first kiss, and moments of accomplishment (such as our graduation or acknowledgement from someone who we respect and admire). Like trauma, these events typically make a long-lasting impression on our psychological landscape. What is it that trauma and fortuity have in common? A few things, it turns out.

The most striking similarity between trauma and fortune is that they are both extremely emotional. Trauma elicits the emotions of fear and anger, as a reaction to a life-threatening event. Fortune, on the other hand, is emotionally charged with joy, elation, and affection. The lesson here is that emotionally charged experiences stick with us. If we are able to make the piece of information emotionally significant, we increase the chances of retaining it.

In the *Levels of Processing Theory* this is called *deep processing*. Instead of encountering information in an impersonal, detached, fashion (*surface processing*), we invest significance into the information in a deep and penetrating way. Research backs this up—the more emotionally-charged the information, the more likely we will remember it.

Another characteristic that trauma and fortune share is that they are *personal*. Love, hate, fear, and joy are not merely emotions; they are soulful reactions to our personal experiences. When something is personally relevant to us, when the information directly affects us, it is processed on a deep level. Making the information personally relevant will make the information stick.

There is one more similarity between the two life events. Trauma and fortune are both *unexpected*. Whether it is the tragedy of a natural event or the wonder of falling in love, both hit us by surprise. There seems to be something about a surprise that makes it more likely to remember. Little research has been done on how to use this effect in studying, but I can offer some suggestions on how to learn by surprise.

In his essay "Nature," Ralph Waldo Emerson teaches us that the natural world is a metaphor for the human mind. Listen to Emerson in his own words:

". . . Have mountains, and waves, and skies, no significance but what we consciously give them, when we employ them as emblems of our thoughts? The world is emblematic. Parts of speech are metaphors, because the whole of nature is a metaphor of the human mind. The laws of moral nature answer to those of matter as face to face in a glass. "The visible world and the relation of its parts, is the dial plate of the invisible." The axioms of physics translate the laws of ethics. . ."

What Emerson described, and my father discovered intuitively, is that we can find insights into our mind from the natural world around us. We just have to learn to speak the language of the poet.

Both the *levels of processing model* and my father's *stream theory* illustrate two main concepts in improving memory of something—it is done through heavy emotional relevance, or through regular, consistent repetition. The research supports this approach. The more time you spend thinking about the information, the more likely you are to remember it.

Researchers in memorization have found a number of techniques that will increase memory through deep processing. I am going to teach these tricks to you, all of which I incorporated into my "A-Effort Study Method" (Chapter 3).

Attention & intention

Something you are going to need to do to improve your memorization skill is to learn a few things about memorization. Notice that I am speaking here about *memorization* and not *memory*. *Memorization* is a verb, an action, a thing that you do. *Memory* is a noun, a thing. I am not so interested in improving your *memory* as I am in improving your ability to *memorize*.

Memorization is the process of integrating new experience with old experience. When we experience something new it is understood (made sense of) against the background of what we already know. How we organized past experience into a meaningful whole, what thinkers call a *worldview* or *perspective*, will determine how we integrate and make sense of something new. In this way, things that we experience take on unique significance to us. For example, the person who desires to write a book will experience an English class differently than the person who has no interest in writing. Our *intention* and past experiences shape how we see and experience new things.

Memorization involves two steps: *encoding* and *storing*. Put in plain English, this means that you have to actively put things into memory (encoding) and secure it there for future use (storing). These are two processes that require *thought*, *planning*, and *attention*—*attention* being the starting point.

Have you ever seen something happen so fast that it did not register in your mind? Sometimes we witness events, like a car accident, that happens so quickly and so unexpectedly, that even though our eyes saw it, our mind did not register it. A similar experience happens when we get to the end of a chapter and realize that although our eyes were reading, our mind was elsewhere, and it is as if we did not read at all.

What these two examples illustrate is the need for *attention* when memorizing. Information will not make it into our memory if we do not actively attend to and *encode* it into our experience. This, the first step in memorization, is often the place where people who claim to have a "bad memory" are sabotaging themselves. Often those very folks, who can't seem to memorize anything, have no problem recalling, with incredible detail, an event that they were *interested* in.

The key here is to become aware that memorization begins with attention. If you haven't already, you must begin training yourself to become a fully engaged reader and listener. This means that you are actively thinking about the information that you are reading, and integrating it into your life. You must develop the skill and stamina to actively engage the text, to fall into it, and to remain completely absorbed within it, in order to commit it to memory.

Here is a personal experiment for you to conduct on yourself. If you do not consider yourself to be someone who enjoys reading, go to your local bookshop and look through the books that are on topics that truly interest you. Maybe it is sports, or fashion, or gaming. Whatever it is that you *love* to do, read through a book or magazine on that topic. At the end of each paragraph, ask yourself what the writer said. If you can say, in your own words, what the author was getting at, you have the kind of attention needed to commit the information to memory. Most likely the information that you read was so useful to you that it is memorized already!

The next part of the experiment involves going to a section of the bookshop or library that you have absolutely no interest in. Go ahead; pick out a book on quilting, baseball, or whatever—just so that it is of absolutely no interest to you whatsoever. Now sit down and begin reading through this book. Are you able to put the paragraphs into your own words? Most of us have difficulty getting through a few sentences of something that does not interest us. That is the beginning of what many dismiss as a "poor" memory.

So here's what we have discovered. In order to effectively *encode* information into our memory we must *attend* to it—*we must pay attention to it*. We naturally pay attention to things that interest us and have consequences for our life. We pay attention to information that is useful to us. When it comes to learning and memorizing, not all of the information is going to appear useful to us. However, we have to be able to memorize it in order to get what does seem useful to us, whether that is a skill, an insight, a grade, or a degree. If you can figure out how to make a thing *useful to your life*, you will greatly increase your ability to memorize it.

The inability to foster interest on demand seems to be an epidemic in modern culture. Maybe it has always been a supreme obstacle for humans? Either way, many of us suffer from a morbid avoidance of thinking. I am not saying this to condescend; I believe that it is more than a mere morality of self-discipline. Experts in the area find that we have evolved to recognize paths of least resistance when thinking and heuristic rules for quick, effective decision-making. However, these quick and dirty habits often come with a cost. Going about life in this way is good for some things, and disastrous for others. Learning takes a great degree of self-discipline, sometimes requiring uncomfortable, effortful motivation. Developing a thick skin for doing things you do not necessarily want to do can garner great benefits in the long run.

The second aspect of memorization, the experts call this *storage*, comes after you have actively attended to the information and are ready to dynamically commit it to memory. Storage has its own characteristics that, once understood, can be used to your benefit to effectively and efficiently memorize.

Emotional significance

As we have already seen, attaching emotional significance to information will greatly increase the depth of processing and memorization. How do you make something emotionally significant? That takes a little work but, as you will see, the work of memorization is a lot like digging; the more you shovel, the deeper you go!

To make thought emotionally significant, try to apply it to something or someone that you know. Maybe a certain theory in psychology helps you to understand your best friend's tendency to always be late for your meet-ups. Perhaps that supply-demand chart from economics explains why that designer's jeans were so much cooler *before* everyone had them. Then there was that ex-girlfriend who always had garlic breath when you kissed, now garlic makes your heart race—she helped you to understand and remember *classical conditioning!* Find a way to associate a meaningful emotion to a concept that you want to remember; you'll find it difficult to forget.

Personal relevance

Closely related to the function of *emotional significance* is *personal relevance*. When a concept or piece of information is personally relevant, it is almost impossible *not to remember it!* Take for example, how I came to memorize (and earn an "A") in my first course on psychological disorders.

At the time I was taking this class, I was hired by the local hospital to work as a mental health technician on its Behavioral Health unit. Working in this setting, I was forming relationships on a daily basis with people who were dealing with the very disorders that I was studying. Each disorder took on a face for me, Juan and depression, Mona and schizophrenia, Paula and bipolar disorder. When exam time came, I simply thought of the people that I had formed relationships with at the hospital. These were no longer isolated, objective, diagnoses; they were sketches of people that I knew.

Personal relevance is closely related to *emotional significance* because things that are personally important to us necessarily elicit emotions. If you really want to remember something, and remember it for good, make it personally relevant.

Visualization

Evolutionary psychologists tell us that humans have a highly evolved propensity for visual memory. As social animals, our ability to remember faces has served as one of the most useful assets in the survival of our species. Our preliterate, visual, ancestors developed a keen visual memory to identify friends and foes.

This acute visual memory survives in us today. In one study, subjects were able to identify faces that they previously encountered for only four seconds, one month later, with over 90% accuracy. Think about that. Having only seen a face for four seconds, we are able to recognize it one month later. That is a testament to our highly evolved visual memory.

As it turns out, we don't need to actually see it to memorize it. Mental visualization activates the same memory areas of the brain as perceptual visualization. But this is nothing new; concert artists have known this for years.

Concert pianist Paul Schocker once told me that the best way to memorize a piece of music was to "play through it," away from the piano. That's right, he recommended playing through the music in one's head, placing the fingers and hands on an imaginary keyboard. Schocker was a master pianist, harpist, and composer who had graduated from the Juilliard School in the 1930s, going on to a long and influential career as a performer and teacher. I believe him on this method—he learned it from none other than Sergei Rachmaninoff.

Closing your eyes and imagining a visual picture of what you are reading will brand it into your mind. One student memorized the major areas of the brain by first closing her eyes and visualizing the labeled brain, carefully reading each label, and later by repeatedly drawing the mental image with pencil and paper.

I believe that visualization in memorization is so effective that I am going to tell you to draw pictures while you are reading, studying, and listening to the lecture. For this I recommend a bound notebook with thick, blank, pages. While you are reading, or listening to a lecture, draw visual schematics about the concepts. A lecture on history can include the interactions of key personalities, along with visual cues about who they are, where and when they were from, and what they were about. The page will come alive with a lively, schematic sketch of the historical event. The act of drawing not only engages the visual memory, but also exercises the *kinesthetic* memory. Still not convinced of the power of sketches? Take a look at Leonardo da Vinci's notebooks.

Organization

When we make sketches (called schematics) we organize the information in a meaningful arrangement. In drawing, the information is symbolically represented by images. How we choose to organize those symbols into meaningful wholes will depend not only on the information we are learning, but how we come to understand it.

There are two general ways of organizing schematics. *Linear* organization typically follows a line, like in a timeline chronology or a step-by-step procedure. *Linear* organization is often used in expository writing, when something is explained in a logical, formulaic way. Linear organization is great for some topics and some learners, but not well suited with others. Take for instance topics that have multiple interpretations, which depend on a theoretical framework.

This type of schematic calls for *nonlinear* organization. *Nonlinear* schematics do not follow a Rube Goldberg, cause and effect linearity, but are more interactionist and chaotic. The dynamic complexity of most phenomenon can only be described in a *nonlinear* way, a model that allows for complicated interaction and what can be called the *feedback-feed-forward loop*. Having difficulty grasping this nonlinear stuff? Don't be surprised; most of our pre-college education tends to offer, straightforward, easy-to-digest *linear* explanations. One reason *nonlinear* is difficult to get is because it has been educated out of us. Neat, *linear* explanations are much more comfortable than complicated *nonlinear* models. Unfortunately, teaching children from an exclusively *linear* approach locks them into a rigid, and often myopic, point-of-view. Getting comfortable with nonlinear organization will open your thinking up to new convergences between topics, that we were taught, had nothing to do with each other.

To "get" the idea of a *nonlinear* schematic (sketch), imagine a root like ginger. The ginger root grows underground and is called a *rhizome*. The thing that makes rhizomes different from typical roots is that there is no center "stalk" and no branches. Whereas traditional schematics depict "trees" that have a central, base, idea with topical "branches," a rhizome grows not from a center, but from nodes. The Internet is a network of interconnected nodes, some larger than others, that has no "center."

A nonlinear schematic might start in several places on your paper, several disparate concepts, which grow in ways that connect in process. The main distinction here is that linear models start with the structure and force the information to fit, whereas nonlinear models start with the information and allows the structure to appear from it. Nonlinear models often look like elaborate works of art, whereas linear models tend to look like tree diagrams. Each has its place in memorization and understanding.

Organization is one of the most important aspects of effective memorization. When we place pieces of information into a meaningful context (called a *Gestalt*), we are more likely to remember it.

The act of organizing the information into a *Gestalt* gives it meaning. In other words, how we organize the information will determine what it means. This is a rather abstract and difficult idea to get, so I'll let Jane, my former student, now a graduate in psychology, explain what I cannot:

> "Imagine that we are all made up of the same organic stuff, DNA. What makes us different is not different DNA, but rather, DNA arranged differently. It is the organization of the stuff, and not the stuff itself, that makes us who we are. Things don't have meaning on their own; they have meaning in relation to other things. If you reorganize these relationships, you change the meaning of the things. That is called the *Gestalt*."

I bow to Jane, and proudly say that she has surpassed her teacher.

Organization also includes integrating information from the lecture with information from the textbook. Most college professors will treat the text as ancillary to the lecture; this means that, unlike high school, what you read in the book will supplement your professor's expertise as a knowledgeable "expert" in the field. Often you will hear little mention of the textbook during the lecture and it will be your job to organize the lecture notes with the text. As we discussed in Chapter 2, it is wise to do the assigned readings *before* the lecture. This will help you to integrate and organize the information outside of class.

When you sit down to do your assigned readings, begin by taking a few minutes to peruse through the lecture notes corresponding to the text that you are reading. By revisiting the lecture notes on a daily basis, you not only increase your exposure to them, you also actively integrate the professor's lecture with the assigned readings. Here's an example.

There was a notoriously complicated French thinker named Jacques Lacan. Lacan's thinking is very difficult and most scholars don't even want to attempt to figure it out. In fact, many either avoid his works or dismiss his writings as impenetrable. Yet, many thinkers *have* penetrated Lacan, because they figured out the *Lacanian code*. What is the secret to reading Lacan? As Lacanian expert Slavoj Zizek, explained it, you can't just read Lacan's writings (called the *Ecrits*), you must simultaneously study the *seminars* (lecture transcripts) too. If you read the writings or the seminars on their own, they make little sense. But when you read the writings with the seminars, *voila!*—the impenetrable becomes penetrable.

Because most college professors will not lecture straight from the book, it is important to organize your lecture notes *with* your assigned readings. Often the lecture only makes sense *after* you have read the background text. Professors assume that you can read the material on your own and bring questions to them during office hours or class or to the TA. Because professors expect that you are reading the text on your own, they may only occasionally refer to it in class. Some students mistakenly take this to mean that the text is not important. The answer to that single most repeated question from students is, "Yes, you do need the book, and you do need to read it on your own!"

Another way in which organization can help memorization (discussed in Chapter 3) is keeping chapter information in the order that it is presented in the textbook or lecture. In other words, organizing the information into a meaningful narrative. Placing the information into a meaningful narrative (storyline) will significantly increase your ability to remember it. For instance, try to memorize the following list of ten words, in order:

Patches

Hold

That

Little

Life

Meaning

Together

Threads

There is no doubt that most people could spend a few minutes repeating these words and committing them to memory. Even so, after an hour or so the words would be forgotten. In the words of Mark Twain, memories are "…little threads that hold life's patches of meaning together." Once the words are organized into a meaningful whole, they cease to be individual pieces of information and become, instead, a piece of meaningful, contextual, thought. The quote by Twain is difficult to forget—even after a single reading.

Before the onset of written text, around four thousand years ago, the tradition of sharing religious and clan histories was oral. This means that without written texts, the histories and stories of a people were spoken from one generation to the next and committed to memory. This is the reason why so much of the oldest histories are organized in psalms, sagas, and elaborate myths. Memorization was not exact; in fact the idea of *verbatim* memory did not enter into our sensibility until after scribes wrote down and *documented* the oral stories. The ancients knew the trick well—putting information into a story will commit it to memory. Add in a deeply held, *emotional*, religious or clan belief with *personal relevance* and you have a powerful memorization cocktail!

Chunking

When we take random words and arrange them into a meaningful whole, we are transforming many, distinct, concepts into one. Think of this in terms of a musical melody. What makes a melody irresistibly, and sometimes irritatingly, unforgettable is the order of the notes, not merely the notes themselves. All of the melodies of the Western music tradition, from folk to classical, jazz to rock, are made up of the same 12 tones, arranged in different ways. Not taking into account tempo, rhythm, and harmony, the 12 tones of the chromatic scale have 479,001,600 possible combinations.

Multiply that by the infinite number of rhythmic, harmonic, and tempo combinations and we have more melodies than we can ever imagine. The point here is that when we sing our favorite songs we are not memorizing individual pitches, but rather, complete, musical sentences (called phrases). The phrase has a meaning making it easy to remember.

When pieces of information are sequenced into a meaningful whole we call it *chunking*. Memory researchers have found that when we chunk information, like *chunked* notes in a melody, we can remember vast amounts of information, accurately and easily. Here are a few everyday examples.

In the US, ten digit telephone numbers are organized into three *chunks* of information: 212-121-2121. Instead of remembering ten, individual, numbers we remember three, meaningful, chunks of numbers. The same is true for social security numbers and other forms of identification. One of the most striking examples of *chunking* is common to most children educated in America. It is the English alphabet song. Because music automatically chunks words into phrases, the "alphabet song" transforms twenty-six individual letters into eight chunks of information. Go ahead, sing the song and count the pauses—all eight of them!

The researcher who turned us on to *chunking* was American psychologist George Miller. In his legendary paper *The Magical Number Seven, Plus or Minus Two*, Miller illustrated how throughout history and cultures, people have naturally organized information into groups of five to nine *chunks*. Memory seems to decline if the information exceeds nine chunks.

How do you organize the material you are studying into chunks? Keeping in mind Miller's *Magical Number Seven, Plus or Minus Two*, you can draw schematics that are arranged in groupings no greater than nine. For example, much of the schematic diagrams used to organize systems in biology use nine or less chunks. One common to my discipline is the diagram for the nervous system, which is organized into eight chunks of information (central, peripheral, autonomic, somatic, afferent, efferent, sympathetic, parasympathetic). When studying course material, try to organize related information into nine chunks or less. This will greatly increase the information's memorizability.

Mnemonics

The ancient Greek and Roman orators, politicians, sophists, raconteurs and philosophers had a method for committing vast amounts of information to memory. It is known as the *method of loci*.

Loci (sounds like low-key) is plural for the Latin *locus*, which means *place* (think *location*). This method was used by anyone who was delivering a speech or lecture to an audience, without notes. Even to this day, the most effective speakers are able to speak freely from inside, without the aid of external notes. The *loci method* works by incorporating visualization with organization. By envisioning a physical space (often your home works well) and organizing your speech by imagining visual cues during an imaginary "walk" through your house, memory is structured. Here is an example.

As a psychology professor I find myself lecturing on certain topics regularly. One of those topics, biological psychology, has a lot of little details that are important to describe to the students. Since it is easy to forget little details, I developed my lectures on biological psychology using *the method of loci*. This is how I did it.

I began by deciding what the most important pieces of information were that *Introduction to Psychology* students would need to know about biological psychology. I took a big sheet of paper and drew three big boxes, which I labeled: "NERVOUS SYSYTEM," "ENDOCRINE SYSTEM," and "GENETICS."

I then wrote in each of the three boxes the single thing that defined each of them—they are each communication systems of the body, each with unique characteristics. In the NERVOUS SYSTEM box I wrote: "fast, electrical, specific." In the ENDOCRINE SYSTEM box I wrote, "slow, chemical, general." In the box marked "GENETICS," I simply wrote "parent to child."

Because I had learned and studied exactly what this meant, (that the nervous system was an *electrical* system in which messages traveled very *fast,* over one-way nerve tracks, to *specific* destinations) I was able to list just three descriptive words in each box. I knew that given those three words, I could discuss their functions accurately.

The schematic being drawn, I now set out to commit it to memory so that I did not have to carry around notes. I started by following the advice of the ancients; I chose a physical place familiar to me.

I first imagined the front door of my house. Eyes closed, I looked at the familiar door and saw, written above the door, the words: "BIOLOGICAL PSYCHOLOGY." I then began my mental walk through my house by opening the door. In the foyer I saw the three doorways that are in the house, one leading to the dining room, one to the kitchen, and one into the basement. Above each door I read: "NERVOUS SYSTEM," "ENDOCRINE SYSTEM," or "GENETICS." Well, I think that you get the point of how the method of loci works. In the NERVOUS SYSTEM room I found three framed pictures hanging on the wall, and so forth.

It took some planning and work, but I managed to arrange my entire lecture as an imaginary walk through my house. After learning it, I could *rehearse* it by simply closing my eyes and walking myself through like a curator. It wasn't long before I could go through the entire lecture, without notes, and not miss a detail. My students had no idea (until now) that I was leading them through an imaginary journey through my house. I hope that they felt like welcomed guests!

Another mnemonic device that I have found useful over the years relates substitute, visually or semantically charged terms together. Known by memory researchers as the *substitute word method*, it relies on substituting new words with similarly sounding (or looking) terms that are familiar. Here is an example.

When I was first learning the four lobes of the brain's cerebral cortex, I was overwhelmed with all of the new information that I had to commit to memory. As any psychology student will tell you, neuroanatomy can be an extremely challenging area of study, requiring a great deal of memorization. I developed a substitute word method that worked so well, that I have taught it to all of my students over the years.

The cerebral cortex is "mapped" into four sections on each half of the brain. The *frontal lobe* is obviously the front part of the brain, but the other three are not so straightforward. The *occipital lobe* is at the back of the brain, whereas the *temporal* and *parietal lobes* are horizontally stacked in the middle.

At the top of the brain, sandwiched between the *frontal* and *occipital lobes* is the *parietal lobe*. *Parietal* sounds a lot like *parental* to me, and parents are always hovering over us, so I linked-up *parietal* with *parental* and remembered that the *parietal lobes* were at the top.

Occipital, to me, sounded like *ox*, which somehow related in my mind to *ass* (like a donkey), which was at the backside. Finally, the *temporal lobes* are located near the temples of the head, which made it tough to forget.

A lesson from classical musicians

Speaking of breaking things up into little chunks, that is exactly what I recommend for duration of memorization time. As we discussed in Chapter 3, too much information at once is like taking a drink from a fire hose. The best way to memorize efficiently, and effectively, is through sipping, not gulping.

According to authorities in the matter, five short, half-hour study sessions are more effective than one long, two-and-a-half hour session. Organizing your study time in briefer chunks with frequent breaks will greatly increase your memory performance.

I have found that this model of memorization is extremely powerful, and would like to elaborate on some personal research that might be of use to you. Using the brief study technique, I have found that I can study one subject for a half-hour, take a few minutes break, and then study a different subject for a half-hour with complete revitalization. Many students have reported to me what I am describing to you. I continuously use this myself—it is not studying or reading that exhausts us; it is studying or reading the same topic that is fatiguing.

I have a rather unusual reading style that only a few of my colleagues and students report sharing. That is, I am typically reading six or seven books at once. I will read half of a chapter in one book, put it aside, and read a half chapter in another book, thereby remaining completely fresh. For some reason I can read for entire days, from different books, for as much as ten hours at a time with little more than a short break here and there. I think that this unusual technique has something to do with my early learning style. Let me explain.

When I first graduated from high school I attended a classical music conservatory in New York City. It was not uncommon to spend at least six hours per day learning, memorizing, and "polishing" etudes, orchestral passages, and solo work. It was in the conservatory practice room that I picked up my habit of switching between multiple pieces in rehearsal.

You see, practicing music, I find, is a lot like studying for an exam. The only difference is that the equivalent of an exam in music, the performance, is in front of an audience, and fails with only one error. Yes, in classical music the stakes are that high.

In conservatory you meet with your teacher once per week for an hour or so. During that hour you are expected to demonstrate your work from the preceding week's practice, and are then assigned new work to be learned in the next week's practice. A classical music student is typically learning two etudes, a number of orchestral excerpts, and a concerto—all at once. This is not including the maintenance (rehearsal) of existing repertoire. Maintaining and polishing repertoire is an ongoing, lifelong process for a musician. The interpretation of a piece early in one's career can be completely different in the later career.

Often practicing a particular piece of music means concentrating on short (only a few measures), extremely difficult, sections. The rule that I was taught, and I found useful, was that after fifteen repetitions of a passage, it was necessary to step away from it—otherwise the attention, concentration, and deliberate thought needed to improve the passage was exhausted. It is not unlike when we find ourselves unable to say what we have just read, because our concentration was worn out.

The trick classical musicians use is to vary the material. We spend the time it takes to make fifteen, meaningful, intelligent, and deliberate passes over a difficult excerpt and then let it rest. We put it away for an hour, or a day, and move on to some other passage. The amazing thing is finding that you can approach fifteen passes on a different excerpt with complete freshness of concentration! The successful results of this are baffling, but neuroscience sheds light on what might be happening.

You see, when we learn something new, the brain actually changes. New learning, whether it is a piece of information or a fingering on the violin or piano, is reflected in the brain by the formation of new neural connections and pathways. Like a bunch of movable wires, neurons progress towards other neurons, making new connections, whenever we learn something new or think differently. This is amazing enough, but the next part is even more astonishing.

If you play an instrument, or practice choreographed dance, you will have experienced exactly what I am about to describe. When we rehearse for only a half of an hour, the neurons develop a growth momentum and continue to move towards the new connections in the hours after we have practiced. It is not uncommon to practice for a half-hour, go to sleep, and wake up able to play the passage with ease. The brain keeps practicing long after you have stopped! Both reading and memorizing seem to be no different. Like musicians, you might find that you can spend long hours studying just by make frequent changes of subject.

Remember, the *level of processing model* informs us that the deeper we process something, the longer we will remember it. The single most effective way to deeply process information is through repetition, what psychologists call *rehearsal*.

Rehearsal

In recent years I have heard a lot of booing and hissing over rote memorization. Learning something by rote is committing it to memory by mechanized, repetitive exposure. This is the old "write it 100 times and you'll learn it" technique. In favor of the equally important ability to holistically integrate and converge conceptual information, rote memorization has been cast as an old-fashioned relic of the Lancasterian teaching method. Maybe it is old-fashioned, but I find it indispensable for college success.

I firmly believe that one needs to memorize some basics before establishing one's own position. What I mean is, just giving your opinion is acceptable in some arenas, but not in college. Academic discussion requires that you have grounding in the topic that you are presenting *your* ideas about. In most instances, learning that information is going to require some highly mechanized, repetitive rote learning.

Remember those music students I described earlier? Long before they were playing concerti and even etudes, they were memorizing scales and arpeggios. You see, most of the music that these musicians learn is made up of musical building blocks like scales and arpeggios. Once musicians have memorized the keys, scales, and arpeggios, they are better equipped to intelligently play the repertoire of their instrument.

How musicians memorize scales is revealing for those who study memory. The first step, before the student picks up the instrument, is to hand write the scales, all twelve of them, from memory. This takes a great deal of determination, concentration, and repetition.

Music students often carry manuscript notebooks around with them to practice writing the scales. Repeatedly manuscripting all twelve keys, until it is done with confidence and ease, is the preliminary step for mastering the scales.

Next, the student begins to commit to memory, one at a time, the playing of the scales on the instrument. Because the theoretical foundation has been committed to memory, through rote learning, the student can focus all of his or her concentration on executing the scale. In other words, *rote learning turns effortful action into effortless habit.* Ever see a pianist hold a conversation while playing a piece? That's the power of turning an action into a habit!

A word of warning is in order. The old saying "practice makes perfect" is a bit misleading. If we practice something incorrectly we will memorize it incorrectly. This is why it is important to remain conscientious when memorizing new material. I would like to suggest a new motto for rote learning: "Perfect practice makes perfect," or better yet, "practice makes *permanent.*"

Elaboration

One of the best methods for sinking information into the deepest levels of memory is to think, talk, and write about it. Psychologists who specialize in memorization call this *elaboration.* The idea here is pretty clear: the more time and effort one spends thinking about, reworking, and critiquing something, the more deeply it becomes processed. Having a simple discussion about a topic greatly increases our capacity to remember it.

My students know an analogy that I use in lecture to describe *elaboration.* I like to compare thinking to eating, in particular the idea that *what* we eat will determine *how* we eat. Let me unpack this thought for you.

If your diet is primarily processed food, that is, food that is prepackaged, de-boned, pre-chewed, and pre-digested, you will become accustomed to eating in a very disengaged and thoughtless way. For example, the typical chicken nugget at the fast food chain requires minimal chewing, no cutting, and can be eaten very quickly.

Chicken patty and hamburger sandwiches are much the same. They truly are *fast foods*, in that they can be eaten very rapidly. Compare these processed foods to the typical cuisine of Europe, Central and South America, Africa, or the West Indies.

In the foods of these cultures the preparation and cooking calls for meat that is not processed and is still on the bone. Not only does cooking meat on the bone add flavor to the dish, it also adds certain nutrients. But there is something else that happens when you prepare meals that include meat that is on the bone–it changes the way you eat the meal.

Our stomach has certain nerve receptors that send a message to the brain when we have eaten enough. Evolutionarily, this feature has evolved with the eating of freshly slaughtered and freshly cooked meat—on the bone. Our evolutionary ancestors did not have processed food.

The pace at which one can eat a meal with bones is much slower than the rate at which we can eat boneless, macerated meat. Because there is a delay between the expanding stomach and the brain getting the message that the stomach is full, we continue to eat for about ten minutes after the stomach has reached capacity. The amount of food that is typically consumed when having to eat around a bone is much less than the amount of fast food consumed. Literally, we are overeating because of the way we are processing our foods.

There is a second issue that comes about from how we eat processed food. These foods typically require little chewing, are easily swallowed, and do not require careful eating. In other words, the predigested texture of the food means that we can eat faster and swallow with less chewing. This results in larger chunks of improperly chewed food in the stomach, which causes indigestion. Again, the body has evolved to process unprocessed food, not the other way around.

What is the analogy with memorization and, specifically, with *elaboration*? Currently most college professors are required by their departments to use a publisher's textbook in a course. Often these textbooks are the equivalent to prepackaged, predigested, "value meals" at the fast food restaurant. The information is pre-chewed, predigested, and ready to consume, often quickly and without thought, by students everywhere.

Only a handful of your professors will still use primary source texts in your classes. That means that instead of reading the original writings of Sigmund Freud, you will be reading someone's presentation of Freud's ideas. The former is akin to eating the meat off of the bone; it takes deliberate and careful consideration, often taking much more time to process and digest. The latter is already chewed for you. Just like little birdies that cannot yet digest food on their own, students get bits of predigested information dropped into their gullets by the "mother bird"—in the form of the college textbook.

By now it should be no surprise that I am not a fan of textbooks—unless they are primary source excerpts, leaving the "chewing" for the student. You see, the act of "chewing" on the text, the act of thinking about it, working it out, and spending time making sense out of it, forces us to process it on a much deeper level. The more we think about something, rework it in our minds, use it, explore it from different perspectives, and elaborate on it—the more likely we are to commit it to our memory.

So how do you elaborate on a topic when studying? Here is the model that I used while taking my college classes. Give it a try in yours.

I treated the textbook as an appetizer. That's right, the textbook chapter was not the main course, but rather, a little, easy to swallow, "taste" that whetted the appetite before the main course. As I read the chapter, having certain studies or ideas presented in easy-to-understand ways, I jotted down the names of the people and their ideas in the margins of the text. After completing the chapter I would go to the library, or on the Internet and search for those names, concepts, articles, and books that I had read *about* in the textbook.

What did I find? Well, often I found that the textbook did a pretty good job at explaining the difficult primary text in a user-friendly way. However, I did not go to college to get user-friendly information. On the contrary, I wanted to be challenged to think my own thoughts, not merely recite the thoughts of others. I also found that textbooks can be very biased and very inaccurate when it comes to introducing other thinkers' work.

Here are just two examples of how textbooks can be inaccurate. Every current introduction to psychology textbook either quotes or presents "Sigmund Freud's Iceberg Model of the Mind." The interesting thing is, when you go to the complete writings of Freud, there is no mention of an iceberg. Another example? Psychology students are taught that Erik Erikson was a "stage" theorist who described the seven "stages" of human development. When I went to the original chapter I found the title "ages" rather than "stages," not to mention an introduction in which Erikson emphatically said that humans do not follow "stages."

Now some might think, "Who cares about this hair splitting; is it really important?" And I reply to those skeptics, "Yes, and all the better for me to remember it!" You see, by going to the original texts, by finding them, holding them in my hands, exploring them, and reading them, I was thinking about the topics in a far more elaborate way. This type of research required a kind of thinking that pushed those basics (the ones presented in the textbook) to such a deep level in my memory that they were there for good.

"Chew" your information carefully, deliberately, and seek out the "meat that is still on the bone." Don't forget to wash it down with some movies though....

Another way to elaborate is actually very fun. I'm talking about video and movie study-night! The point of *elaboration* is to stimulate thought about the topic you are studying. Because reading has no privileged position in how we elaborate (some research even shows that we learn better from listening and watching), we can elaborate through many media, including videos, audio recordings, websites, and films. The point is that you are spending time looking into and exploring the ideas that you want to memorize.

One of the courses that I teach in media theory investigates how the media industries influence how we spend money, how we vote, how we view the world, and even how we view ourselves. This is a fascinating and timely topic to read about, but even more engaging can be the multimedia venues that illustrate it.

There are numerous documentaries, films, television and radio shows, and websites devoted to media, culture, and society. By entering your topic of study into the popular search engine you can find yourself going through dozens of sites that are presenting the concepts from your textbook, in dozens of different ways. Before you know it, hours will have passed and you will have been so engrossed in the information that you might think that you forgot to study.

But, this is studying. As long as you are investigating the concepts that you want to learn, you are elaborating, regardless of the medium. So to prepare for your next exam, make sure that you watch some good movies!

Jennifer, a senior, psychology major at Rutgers University, gives a final warning on *thoughtless* memorization:

"Memorization alone will not do it. Your brain will not process these ideas and concepts into your Long Term Memory and it is likely that you will encounter them again. Save yourself some time and *learn* your material because it will pay off in the end."

7 THE OUTLOOK FOR SUCCESS

"As long as a man stands in his own way,
everything seems to be in his way."
-Ralph Waldo Emerson

The Zen of academics

I have a model for academic success that I learned from the ancient Buddhist texts. I call these the *Four Noble Truths of College*. They go something like this:

I.   College is difficult, it necessarily involves suffering.
II. The basis of difficulties in college is habits.
III. You can reduce difficulties with the right habits.
IV. Practice the habits of successful students.

Although this is a somewhat humorous take on the Four Noble Truths of the Buddha, it is also a tried and true outlook for success in college. If you can accept that college is going to be difficult and that you can control the majority of the difficulties through good habits, you will be on your way to college success.

At the foundation of this approach is the right attitude towards yourself and your studies. The more time you spend cultivating this attitude and these habits, the more likely you will find peace of mind, a sense of accomplishment, and a unfailing sense of satisfaction.

Fall in love

I remember feeling frustrated, hopeless, and angry at having another teacher tell me that I was doing poorly in his class. Being a thirteen year-old junior high school student, I turned to my friend, an "A" student, for help. "What can I do to get better grades?" I pleaded. Davy simply whistled a tune from Disney's *Snow White and the Seven Dwarfs*, "Whistle While you Work."

We laughed and went on with our day, but his response stuck with me. Looking back I think this might have been the moment that I learned how my attitude towards what I am doing determines how well it is done.

Believe me when I tell you this: *attitude is everything*. The first thing you must do, when faced with a class, assignment, project, or requirement that you absolutely abhor is to fall in love with whatever it is that you have to do. Along the way to earning a college degree there will be numerous requirements that you will be expected to accomplish in order to graduate. What is the healthful and beneficial attitude to take here? *Do whatever it takes, and love doing it!* That's right, figure out how to turn "loathe it" into "love it."

Sounds impossible? The truth is, it really isn't that difficult to find a way to overcome dislike for something. It is often a matter of how we are approaching or viewing the thing that needs to be changed. Psychologists call this *cognitive reframing*. It works something like this.

Say that you are required to complete two semesters of statistics in order to graduate with your degree in counseling psychology. Okay, what does mathematical statistics have to do with psychotherapy? Actually, today, it does have something to do with it. You are going to have to get through these two courses in order to get what you want—a degree in psychology. Knowing that you are going to do better, and have less angst, if you convince yourself that you are interested in statistics, you can start by resigning yourself to the fact that you must take the classes. Next, you need to soul search, and I mean serious searching, to find some usefulness for learning the material in the class. This is *reframing*, literally redefining the thing you dislike in order to change the way you feel towards it. Sounds tough? It can be.

Begin by asking your professors what it is about the class that makes it so important to your field of interest. You may discover that studying and learning the topic will be of great benefit to you in your profession. Another approach is to find a way in which the topic or information you are studying may be useful to you in the future. Faced with the statistics issue, the future psychologist might tell herself that she has to learn about statistics so she can recognize when researchers are not being forthright with their claims (as can happen in pharmaceutical marketing). In this way our young therapist is viewing herself as a patient-advocate who is empowered with the insight into "how figures don't lie, but liars figure."

A simple change in perspective can turn the most dreaded requirement into the most memorable and influential learning experience. Take, for example, a class that I needed to complete in *behavioral* psychology. Although I am not so convinced or interested by much of the research or theories proposed by behaviorism, I knew that I needed to complete the course in order to get what was important to me, a degree in psychology. How did I handle it? I used *cognitive reframing.*

You see, instead of kicking, screaming, and complaining I sat down and reasoned how this was going to benefit me in the future. The answer was not only effective; it turned out to be true. I told myself that one day, as a college professor, I might be required to teach this subject to students. That did it! I wanted to be a college professor so badly that my enthusiasm for teaching trumped my apathy for behaviorism. Incidentally, I was offered the opportunity to teach this course at a major university, which not only paid my bills, but also resulted in a longstanding professional relationship. "Why hire me?" I asked the director of the program. "Because you were the only candidate who really liked what you were teaching." Imagine that circle of fate!

So, the next time you have to complete a project that you would rather eat worms than do, remember Snow White's (and Davy's) advice for getting it done, and doing your best job—*whistle while you work!*

What a grade measures

I have never felt that grades meant more than that a person learned how to "play the game" of academics. Truthfully speaking, some of the best-performing students have also been some of the most unenthusiastic thinkers. On the other hand, some of the students who don't perform so well on exams have been particularly intellectual. The "A" student has mastered the number one quality needed to be an "A" student—conscientiousness.

The stories of the geniuses that were mediocre students are all too familiar to repeat here. They do, nonetheless, illustrate that grade point averages are not indicative of intellect, innovation, or creativity. Some of the most celebrated innovators of our day either dropped out of college or were academic underachievers.

Remaining organized, completing assignments on time, attending and participating in class, reading, and studying are all qualities of the *conscientious* student. Since most college textbooks are written for the person of average intelligence, it should be manageable for any college student who is conscientious and dedicated to do well.

Remember, an "A" does not mean that you are a genius, and a "C," "D," "B," or an "F" does not mean that you are not brilliant. Grades are a reflection of *conscientiousness*, not intellect.

It is not all up to you

As an undergrad I had a history class that I found intensely compelling and interesting. The professor, an old-school type who had studied at Columbia University back in the 1940s, was one of the most interesting and stirring lecturers I have had. I was so excited about that history class that I even flirted with changing my major. Then the test came back, "B-."

As the president of the honors society, I was baffled at how this could be. I had earned "A's" in physics and biology, and all of the most challenging courses in my major. How could I have received a "B-" in this introductory history class? I learned very quickly that I had to be satisfied with the effort that I put forth, because when it comes to taking tests, it's not completely in one's own hands.

A common misconception of our culture is that we can control everything—*if only we try hard enough*. I am here to tell you: this a bunch of hooey. You cannot, no matter how hard you try, completely control the outcome of *everything*—including tests and papers.

If you noticed, the title of the book is *An "A" Effort*. This is what you can control, how much *effort* you put into preparing for and taking the exam, or writing the paper.

Other than that, the outcome is out of your hands. Let me explain.

Before becoming a professor I was a student for many years. Not including my twelve years schooling before college, I have been in university for an additional 12 years. That's two undergraduate and three graduate degrees. If there is one thing that I can tell you, it is that not all teachers know how to make a test, or grade a paper. In fact, your professor may never even see your paper or the exam that you are taking, many of which are graded and designed by teaching assistants. At smaller colleges, though, professors do read each paper and make each test.

Some professors do not make the effort to construct test questions in a clear way. Multiple-choice questions sometimes have answers that are so subtle that the professor themselves has trouble answering correctly. You can study, master, and know the material inside out, and still have a poorly written exam that reflects on *your* grade. This is out of your control.

How do you handle a situation in which you know the material but the professor's exams are terribly written? Don't get involved with them in the first place. Unless they are a first-year professor, past students will have reported their experience on websites or evaluation forms. Ask around; get the scoop on the professor. Stay away from professors who give what are considered to be excessively difficult exams. They are unnecessary and damaging to learning.

What you can control is your conscientious effort in the class. If you have put your all into preparing for an exam, I mean have really dedicated yourself to your greatest ability, then you will have a sense of accomplishment regardless of the grade. What matters is that you did your best.

Writing papers is no different. All professors have their own stylistic preferences and their own intellectual biases that they cannot escape. There are, however, professors who truly demand that you develop your writing to its highest level. It is not uncommon for professors to withhold assigning "A's" on midterm papers so that the student has something to work towards on the final paper. Most professors will insist that your writing is outstanding in order to receive an outstanding grade, but some can be unreasonably harsh.

No doubt I will be getting some hate mail from those very same professors I speak of over the previous comments. That's okay. I know, and so should you, that a well-researched and well-written paper should receive an above average grade. But the point is that the grade is not completely in the hands of the writer; it is a dance with the professor who is grading it.

Another consideration to keep in mind is your professors' academic worldview. What is their writing style and theoretical position on the topic you are researching? If they are a professor, then they will have published writing available to read. Taking the time to read a few of their texts will help you to understand how to write an "A" paper for that professor. Remember, the grade takes two people, not just you!

Forget about grades

"Okay," you are thinking, "This guy writes a book about becoming an 'A' student, and then concludes by telling me to forget about grades—what gives?" That is exactly what I am saying. Forget about your grades.

At the end of the day what is important is that you become deeply impassioned about *what* you are learning, so much so that you are reading, studying, and writing because you want to learn about the topic, not because you are required to learn it for a test. Forget about the grade and get fully enmeshed in the excitement of learning. If you do this, the "A" will take care of itself!

ABOUT THE AUTHOR

Dr. Matthew Tyler Giobbi is a lecturer of psychology at Rutgers University, Newark, New Jersey. He is the Erich Fromm Research Associate at the European Graduate School in Switzerland. Dr. Giobbi studied at The New School for Social Research, NYC, and at the European Graduate School in Switzerland.

94184317R00061

Made in the USA
Lexington, KY
25 July 2018